THE FIVE SILENT YEARS
OF CORRIE TEN BOOM

The
Five Silent Years
of Corrie ten Boom

PAMELA ROSEWELL MOORE

ZondervanPublishingHouse
Grand Rapids, Michigan

A Division of HarperCollinsPublishers

The Five Silent Years of Corrie ten Boom

Requests for information should be addressed to:
Zondervan Publishing House
Grand Rapids, Michigan 49530

Library of Congress Cataloging in Publication Data

Rosewell Moore, Pamela.
The five silent years.

1. Ten Boom, Corrie. 2. Christian biography—Netherlands. I. Title.
BR1725.B6724R67   1986   269'.2'0924   [B]   85-26350
ISBN 0-310-61121-0

Credit is gratefully acknowledged for "My Life Is Like a Weaving" by Grant Colfax Tullar, quoted in Chapter 3, and to Christian Literature Crusade, Fort Washington, Pa., for permission to quote from *A Prisoner and Yet. . . .* in Chapter 9.

Edited by David Hazard
Designed by Ann Cherryman

Printed in the United States of America

95 96 97 98 / DH / 19 18 17 16

CONTENTS

ACKNOWLEDGMENTS

The following pages describe the final years of the life of Corrie ten Boom and some of the glimpses I had into the mysteries of life and death.

She and those of us privileged to serve her were the recipients of much love and practical help during the five years of Tante Corrie's illness. So many were the givers of the help that they are largely unnamed in this book.

To them and to John Sherrill, David Hazard, and Jane Campbell, whose editorial gifts helped me to express the lessons of the silent years, I want to extend very deep gratitude.

1.

A Time to Plant

My Work with Tante Corrie Begins

"There is a time for everything, and a season for every activity under heaven."   Ecclesiastes 3:1

It was early spring in 1976 as I drove west toward the city of Haarlem, Holland, a bunch of yellow tulips in the otherwise empty passenger seat beside me in the small French car. The wind was blowing, as it always does in the lowlands, stirring the new, light green growth on the straight rows of poplar trees intersecting the flat countryside. I was aware of the extraordinary light that is peculiar to Holland—caused perhaps by the large expanse of sky in the absence of hills. This brightness, it is said, inspired the Dutch painters, famous for their use of light. I opened the car window a few inches. The air was fresh and cold and smelled of spring. A feeling of new beginnings was in the air. And since the surprise phone call a few days earlier, I wondered if there was to be a new beginning for me, too.

Traffic was light, leaving me time for reflection. Ever since arriving in The Netherlands from my home in England more than seven years before, I had been fascinated by the Dutch. It had been necessary to learn their language and that was a challenge. Whereas the British would have been more likely to try to spare the feelings of those struggling with a new language, the Dutch, in my first year in the country, had

often greeted my efforts to pronounce their guttural conso-
nants and learn their expressions with shouts of honest
laughter. You always knew where you were with them.

They invariably described their character as *eigenwijs*
(stubborn), and they pronounced the word with considerable
pride. I liked them very much and I loved my exciting work
with a mission organization whose principal purpose was to
take Bibles behind the Iron Curtain. Life in Holland had
been a challenge and an adventure for me up until this point.

And now, after working with that mission for seven-and-
a-half years, I was on my way to an interview that would
possibly lead to another kind of work. Corrie ten Boom, 83
years old, had asked me to come to her home in a suburb of
Haarlem to talk with her. She was looking for another
companion, as Ellen de Kroon, who had been with her nearly
nine years, was leaving to be married. It had been some time
since I had last seen Tante Corrie (*Tante*, pronounced tahn-
tuh, is the Dutch word for *aunt*), but we were not strangers,
for upon my arrival in Holland she had been one of the first
people I had met. "Child," she had said, "my home is your
home. You are always welcome here." I had taken her at her
word and had been to visit her during her short stays in The
Netherlands in the following years. She spent most of her time
outside the country as a "tramp for the Lord," to use her
words, but during our brief encounters I had grown to love
and respect her and was able to help her from time to time.

The straight rows of poplar trees, like long plumes,
flashed past the windows. Countryside was turning to town.
It would not be long now before I entered Haarlem, and I
had to admit to mixed feelings. Although on the one hand the
feeling of new adventure was in the air, I doubted that I was
a suitable candidate for the role of companion.

Corrie ten Boom—how well did I really know her? She
was a world figure who had hidden Jews during the Nazi

occupation of Holland and was put in prison and concentration camp for doing so. Had that brave action made her who she was? What made Corrie, Corrie? What had her early years been like?

As I approached Haarlem, the Saint Bavo Cathedral dominated the skyline and looked sedately down on the centuries-old, busy little city. This was the town in which Corrie had grown up—in the happy home of watchmaker Casper ten Boom, his wife Cor, Corrie's two sisters, Betsie and Nollie, and a brother, Willem. She had been born in Amsterdam on April 15, 1892, and could trace her family tree through at least eight generations to 1647 when Jan ten Boom lived at Ruurlo. In 1844 an event took place that was most unusual for its time. Corrie's grandfather, Willem ten Boom, started a prayer meeting for Jewish people. Tante Corrie often referred to it as "a not-to-be-understood answer to my family's prayers for the Jews, for exactly one hundred years later God allowed my whole family to be arrested for their part in saving Jewish people during the Second World War."

Her relationship with the God of her forefathers began at an early age. I had often heard her refer to it. "At five years of age I asked the Lord Jesus to come into my heart," she said, "and He came, and He has never let me down."

I had now passed the city limits. Traffic was becoming thicker and I had to negotiate the busy streets of Haarlem carefully. Just a few yards from where I was driving, but out of sight, was the Barteljorisstraat. It was to this street, near the cathedral, that the Ten Boom family moved from Amsterdam.* Their home was called "the Beje" (pronounced bay-yay) for short, the name consisting of the initial letters of Bartel Joris, Joris being a fourteenth-century inhabitant of the town of Haarlem.

**Ten is capitalized when used without a first name.

The Beje was small and, throughout Corrie's childhood, was full of people—the six family members and three aunts, sisters of her mother, Cor. It was, as Tante Corrie described it, full of color, warmth, music, and laughter, and Mother ten Boom always had room for guests at her table. The home had a solid spiritual foundation. The Bible was read daily. A favorite Dutch national pastime is talking, and there was lots of communication and close family unity in the Beje. Corrie constantly looked for ways to share the love and sense of belonging with which she grew up. As a young woman she started several clubs, including a Christian Girl Scout movement called "The Triangle Girls" and clubs for the mentally retarded.

Had her extraordinarily supportive family background with its many generations of good Dutch Reformed stock made Corrie ten Boom the woman she was? Corrie's mother died when Corrie was still in her twenties; her brother Willem and sister Nollie married; and after the demise of the three aunts, only Casper ten Boom, Betsie, and Corrie were left in the Beje when war broke out. Though they were already middle-aged and older, Corrie, her sister, and father had certainly not been afraid to take the consequences of their convictions when war came. On February 28, 1944, all the Ten Booms were betrayed by a fellow Dutchman who knew they were hiding Jews in the Beje, and were taken to the Haarlem Police Station.

From that place began a horrifying journey. They were transferred to prison in Scheveningen, Holland, where Corrie saw her father for the last time. He passed away after ten days of imprisonment. Most of the family was released, but Kik, Willem's son, died in concentration camp in Germany in his early twenties, and Willem died at the age of 60 in 1946 as a result of an illness contracted in prison. Corrie and Betsie were sent first to a concentration camp at Vught, Holland, then to the dreaded Ravensbruck concentration camp in Germany, which Corrie called "the deepest hell that man can create." Betsie died there on Christmas, 1944, at age 59.

In Ravensbruck, Corrie and Betsie took every opportunity to tell the women prisoners about the love of God. They had been able to smuggle a Bible into the camp with them, and held daily Bible studies. I had heard Corrie say that imprinted on her mind was a picture of her sister, Betsie, sitting in the filthy barracks, surrounded by prisoners, reading to them from the Bible. As she read, a shaft of light from the window fell on Betsie, and Corrie said that it was like a painting by Rembrandt. Frail, older than Corrie by seven years, Betsie was being used by God in those dirty and degrading circumstances. Then Betsie became ill, but her faith was as strong as her body was weak. She said, "Corrie, when the new year comes, we will both be free. God has given me a vision. We must go around the world and tell everyone who will listen the truth that we have discovered here, that there is no pit so deep the love of God is not deeper still."

When the new year came, they were indeed both free. Betsie died and went to be with the Lord; Corrie, having been released from Ravensbruck "by a clerical error of man and a miracle of God," returned to The Netherlands. From there she embarked on a ministry that was to take her to a total of sixty-four countries in thirty-three years.

As I bypassed the town center, it was raining lightly. I headed the car to the suburb of Haarlem called Overveen where Tante Corrie lived. I wondered how I, a rather independent English woman in my early thirties, could possibly blend my lifestyle with that of a determined Dutch lady more than fifty years my senior. Was I cut out to be a companion? I did not look at myself as the companion type.

My mind flitted momentarily to a remark that was passed a few nights earlier. On receiving Tante Corrie's request for an interview, I had been to visit a good friend, a Dutch girl who was about to become engaged and who also knew Tante Corrie well. We prayed together almost every week, and on that night we prayed, in Dutch, that God would show me if it was right to become Corrie ten Boom's companion.

At the end of our prayer time my friend said, in English, "Pam, these words came into my mind: *Till death us do part.*" I recognized them, of course, as part of the marriage ceremony, and I thought, startled: *Surely they don't apply to me and Tante Corrie's request. I don't think I could handle such a commitment for more than a few months.* My friend surely had those words on her mind for the more obvious reason of her engagement.

The long, straight Julianalaan stretched out in front of me, bordered on both sides by bicycle paths. The cyclists had their heads down, bracing themselves against the rain and the wind blowing off the nearby North Sea.

Pulling up to the curb, I parked the car and walked along the tree-lined street, its solid, well-kept houses shining with high-gloss paint, the gardens planted in the uniform Dutch pattern, tidy, clean, and welcoming. Approaching number 32, a three-story house that had been Corrie's base since the previous year, I walked up the stone pathway to the front door. To my right was a square lawn with a golden rain tree that would bloom prolifically later in the year.

A few seconds after my ring, Ellen de Kroon, a tall, blonde woman, answered and I stepped into the warm, welcoming atmosphere of "Agape House." Tante Corrie had named the house after one of the Greek words for "love."

"Let me take your coat," said Ellen, nodding toward the stairway. "Please go up to Tante Corrie. She's having a rest day in bed. I have made some tea and I'll bring it in a moment." Then she disappeared into the kitchen.

As I began the steep climb, I thought how unusual it was

for an 83-year-old woman to choose a home with no downstairs bedroom. The stairs looked rather perpendicular to me even at 32, and I thought it typical of Tante Corrie's energetic spirit that she would be willing to tackle them at least once a day. As I mounted the steps, clutching the bunch of yellow tulips, the questions that had been swirling at the back of my mind caught up to me. Who was I to consider taking on the work of a companion, even for a limited time? Companionship meant being in somebody's presence, or near it, for twenty-four hours of every day. Although I respected Corrie ten Boom, the prospect was rather daunting.

However, I reminded myself, this was only an interview. There would be plenty of time to seek God's further guidance before I decided.

I knocked on the bedroom door and a warm, clear voice told me to come in. On a low double bed, Tante Corrie sat propped with pillows, in pale yellow pajamas. Her silver-gray hair fell to her shoulders, and she was surrounded by paper. I gave her the yellow tulips, and she invited me to sit.

Ellen had followed on my heels with the tea tray, and I was grateful for a moment to orient myself before my interview. I could not help but notice the bright, colorful room.

It was large, with French windows leading onto a balcony. Tante Corrie obviously loved pictures. She had hung as many as wall space would allow. Some were original paintings in oil or watercolor. Some were reproductions, others were photographs. There was a reproduction of Rembrandt's painting of the Lord Jesus with the two disciples whom He had accompanied to Emmaus. There was one of a woman drawing water from a well. The item that drew my attention most was a rectangular plaque with a pink background and the words in Dutch, *My times are in Your hands*.

Tante Corrie took the opportunity of Ellen's coming to hop out of bed and hurry about gathering letters for Ellen to post. Her strength and agility were really surprising. There was no hint of any stiffness. It did not look to me as though she was really resting during this day in bed, but rather making the fullest use of it.

Ellen left, and resettling herself against the pillows, Tante Corrie looked at me with her blue, discerning eyes. There were no opening gambits.

"Well, child, what has the Lord told you?"

"I am willing to help you, Tante Corrie," I ventured, by way of a start.

"Praise the Lord, that is settled then."

I was a little stunned. There was no discussion about hours, wages, holidays, or visits home to my family in England. To Tante Corrie the matter was settled.

"I am nearly 84 now," she continued with much enthusiasm, "and I am at a crossroads in my life. I have asked the Lord to give me a new ministry and I believe He will do it. I do not know what it is yet, but He will show me."

I thought I might interrupt, clarifying my feelings; yet something in her spark and drive captivated me. I held my thoughts.

"When a person is 83 years old," Tante Corrie beamed, "and is able to do just a little bit of the work she loves, that is a great privilege. But I am able to do so much." Pausing, she eyed me, kindly but with firmness. "Child, I am very glad you are going to be my new fellow tramp, but you must know that you will always have the second place. The work comes first."

Quite a statement, I thought, impressed immediately by her unusual honesty. *I'll never be able to say that I was not warned.* And I could see she was not going to pull the wool over my eyes at any time. But a slight wariness nudged me. Surely there could be some uncomfortable situations if the work really always came first.

"We go to the United States at the beginning of April," she declared. "There are some exciting months coming up." She explained that an old chest had come to light that had been lost for many years. It contained old family papers and letters written by her great-grandfather, grandfather, and father. She would be using the material as background for a book she was writing about Father ten Boom, on which she would be working with a nephew in Switzerland. From there we would go on to the United States, where Corrie would be speaking in various places. "The whole journey will take about seven months," she concluded matter-of-factly.

Seven months! I thought. *However could an older person stand up to a seven-month journey? Furthermore, how would I be able to take it?* I managed a polite nod.

Completely undaunted, she continued: "You will love America. In Germany when I worked there after the war I learned how to think. In America I learned how to live. But most important, the people there are in need of the Lord Jesus."

I knew that her book, *The Hiding Place*, and the movie that followed it had brought her many invitations to speak. People everywhere loved "Tante Corrie" as if she were their own dear aunt or grandmother. But I still did not see how I was going to fit into all this.

After a time of prayer and a meal together, the interview ended. As I retraced my steps to the parked car, I buttoned my coat against the wind. As often as the heavy evening traffic gave me opportunity, I thought about the interview. Tante Corrie had been quite settled in her mind that it was right for me to be her companion. I felt a kind of peace about it. But nothing like her sureness, though I knew her well enough to know she would never act presumptuously or force a decision upon me.

Yet Tante Corrie seemed to act with utter certainty, with a sense that all her days were ordered and she had only to listen for God's instructions and follow them. That marvelous things happened as she lived this simple, obedient life seemed the proof that He was behind her. How could I learn to live like that?

How that lady enjoys her work, I thought. *She'll wear me out; I can see it already!*

I only hoped I would be able to help her over the next few months in the right way.

Corrie ten Boom seemed to have an enormous capacity to achieve, a God-given ability to catch a vision and then translate it into reality. I began to look forward to learning from her. But for some reason I went over the bedroom scene of the interview many times. That strong, agile movement of Tante Corrie's as she raised herself from her low bed was etched sharply in my mind. How vividly I was to recall it later, in a different country, a different bedroom, and in very different circumstances.

Even now, though, I was concerned about her age and health. I had heard that her doctor kept a close eye on her heart, though it didn't appear that she had any intention of slowing her pace.

We'll leave things as they are for now, I mused. *I will view this seven-month trip as a sort of trial period. I can always back out later when a more suitable candidate for the role of companion comes along.*

I could not have known, that evening in March as I sped homeward, past the Dutch landscape from which the miraculous light had dissolved into dusk, that I would witness Corrie's most unusual season of ministry. In fact, it would be far different from any of the activities that are normally thought of as ministry.

And how could I have known then that I was about to catch a glimpse behind the opaque windows of time into eternity?

I simply drove, taking comfort in the knowledge that God always seemed to honor Tante Corrie's decisions. I would think of this time as a spring season—a time for "planting" new experiences. Whatever lay ahead for both of us, I was sure that the harvest was in God's hands.

2.

Flexibility

A few weeks after the interview, I was standing again on the doorstep of "Agape House," this time with my suitcases in hand. With the seven-month trial period in mind, I had not closed up my home in central Holland where I had been working, because accommodations in this densely populated country were always hard to come by. I had arranged to have a co-worker live in my small apartment during my absence— just in case.

In fact, as I stood waiting for someone to answer my knock, I felt less certain about my new position than I had on the day Tante Corrie pronounced the matter settled. While I had packed and made my arrangements, I had had time to think, and the facts, as they stood, did not point to Corrie's conclusion.

None of the experiences in my life up until then led me to think that I was a good choice to be the companion of an elderly woman. I grew up in Hastings, East Sussex, on the south coast of England in a closely knit family with a younger sister and brother. My father was a local government officer, my mother a registered nurse, and I had had nothing more than the normal contact with elderly grandparents.

On the contrary, most of my work had been with young people. Moving away from England in my early twenties, I volunteered for a Christian mission in Kenya for one year, and for the next eight years, I had kept a hectic pace working with active, energetic young people of many nationalities—

just the sort of work I loved. As the door opened, I concluded that if I was to be Tante Corrie's companion, I could not look to my past experience for help.

Ellen greeted me again, ushering me inside with her characteristic warmth. She had a flair for making people feel welcome, and I would certainly need her help since she had been Tante Corrie's traveling companion for the previous nine years. I would have to absorb all I could from her before her work ended and mine began in just over a week. The time seemed so short and the amount of information I needed so great. I could not imagine, as Ellen helped me carry my things up the steep stairs to my third-floor room next to Ellen's and a small office, how it all would get done.

After heaving my belongings onto the bed for the moment, we made our way downstairs. I calmed myself with the decision that I would take one step at a time. That decision was well-made, because Tante Corrie met me on the first floor with an announcement that was a little overwhelming.

Welcoming me warmly, she lost no time, but promptly outlined our travel plans. The first stop was Geneva, Switzerland, where she would be working with her nephew on the book about her father, on to New York for a business meeting with her publisher, then to Miami for her first speaking engagement. "We are going to eighteen cities in all," Tante Corrie announced proudly.

I had known, of course, that her travel plans were extensive—but *eighteen cities*. I felt a sinking feeling. I looked at Ellen, hoping that my brief training would be thorough.

With my typical careful logic, I decided to examine the situation one bit at a time. First, I decided, I needed to discover how each day was spent, to learn the routine.

The very next day, I learned that mornings began with a

cup of tea. Tante Corrie, Ellen, and I read together from the Bible and prayed. We prayed particularly for those projects foremost in Tante Corrie's mind—the book and the approaching Easter sunrise service in Miami, also for world situations and for personal matters. What impressed me at once was the simple way she prayed, as though she were holding a conversation with a visible person. Tilting her face upward, eyes closed, she opened her hands palms-up as if the Lord might simply place the answer there.

Observing was one thing. Becoming more personally involved was another. The morning came when, having watched Ellen a couple of times, it was my turn to fix Tante Corrie's very fine, silvery hair, which she wore arranged in a roll around her head.

I felt all thumbs. After all, most women tend to be fussy about their hair, and I was not overly handy as a "beautician." She bowed her head, and I began timidly. Close up, I could not help but compare the two of us. She looked well, I thought, and soft olive-toned skin had a healthy glow. My skin was fair, as English skins often are, without much color. Even seated, I could tell that Corrie must have been a tall woman in her younger days, probably as tall as I. Now her shoulders were a little stooped. I wondered, as I slipped the last pins and the hairnet into place, if Corrie's fine hair had once been as long, thick, and dark as mine was.

She slipped her gold-rimmed glasses on, barely gave a glance in the mirror and said graciously, "Thank you very much. It looks very nice." Rising, she made for her desk. It was a great encouragement—and a relief.

In those first few days together I witnessed an amazing paradox in Corrie. She had the ability to work very intently and yet in a most relaxed way. Although the work—arrangements for forthcoming meetings, research for the book, counseling in person, over the phone, or by letter, television, radio interviews—always had priority, she handled it all without tension. I was astounded at the work that went on, and the many people who crossed the threshold of "Agape House" during that week.

Yet, there always seemed to be time for laughter. Like good Europeans, we stopped for coffee at mid-morning and tea at mid-afternoon. "Let's put the kettle on," Corrie would say, in such a way that it sounded as if it were not really allowed. We left our mound of papers to drink coffee or tea and enjoy a piece of Dutch or Swiss dark chocolate. There is a word often used in the Dutch language and English is the poorer for not possessing it. *Gezellig* means the atmosphere of togetherness that one experiences, for instance, sharing together near a crackling fire, drinking coffee with music in the background. During those first few days with Corrie, I began to enjoy these "gezellig" times.

And yet, as I had feared, living in close proximity like that began to expose some rough edges. For instance, Corrie seemed to have no secrets, always speaking frankly about all aspects of her work and personal life. And she desired that I be equally as frank with her. Of course, I was impressed when she asked, with genuine interest, about my family in England and my friends, but being open voluntarily was not always that easy for me. Corrie liked to open the mail herself and pass on the letters to me to read. I, in turn, shared with her my personal letters. If we were going to work and live together under such intense conditions, it was plain that we would have to begin to pray together about news, both good and bad, that a day's mail might bring.

And it was with prayer that we ended our days. Before Tante Corrie went to sleep, her prayer with me always included these words: "Father, will You keep us so close to Your heart that even our dreams are peaceful, and that we see things as it were more and more from Your point of view."

Shortly before the planned departure, Tante Corrie began packing for the long journey. Here I caught a glimpse of her very pragmatic side. We were in her bedroom and placed the suitcases on her low double bed. For the first time I saw some of the things that the long years of traveling had taught her. It was of great importance to her that we be ready in plenty of time to prevent a last-minute rush. Between us we had seven pieces of luggage, including small and large cases. She asked me to count the luggage carefully as it was loaded at the airport, and again upon arrival. We began by packing her items, and I noticed that she worked methodically, never pausing to ponder or worry that she might forget something important. She was a seasoned veteran of the road in every sense. Last of all, she packed a copy of the New Testament paraphrased by J.B. Phillips, right at the top of a small bag for easy access. Judging by its rather worn black cover, it looked as if it had accompanied her on many journeys.

At one point Tante Corrie packed a folded piece of shiny blue material with yellow threads hanging from it. I asked if it was some embroidery to occupy her during idle moments.

"No, child," she replied, her blue eyes alive with some secret, "this is what I call 'the crown.' You will see how I use it later." Saying no more, she slipped it into a cloth bag.

Next we climbed to my room and took out my suitcases. Tante Corrie looked thoughtfully at the few items I had laid out on the bed for packing. "Do you have any dresses in bright colors?" she asked. "They would suit you very well."

"Just this one, Tante Corrie," I replied, fingering a red dress, trimmed with blue. All my other clothes were rather somber in color.

"When we have time," she smiled, "we will see about getting you some more clothes, things that will be suitable for your new life. That will be fun."

Perhaps the most intriguing thing to me was the way

that Corrie simply refused to be rushed or anxious. We were just days away from a major trip, with so much left to accomplish, when she and Ellen told me that they had set aside one full evening to entertain several of the "club girls," that is, some members of the youth clubs Corrie had run in the early decades of the 1900s. Although I was eager to see that our arrangements were in order, there was nothing to do about it. Everything would grind to a halt for an evening, and I looked forward to meeting these women of another era.

It was an evening of lightheartedness, laughter, of memories without morbid nostalgia. We were seated in the downstairs sitting room, a cozy fire in the grate and the soft light glowing on a portrait of Casper ten Boom. Someone mentioned that the clubs had always operated with four rules, and one guest began searching her memory to recall them. Without hesitation, Corrie listed them: "Seek strength through prayer; be open and trustworthy; bear your difficulties cheerfully; and develop the gifts that God gave you." The rules were fresh in her mind. Nor had she forgotten details about the lives of her guests. Mostly, she talked radiantly about her plans for the future.

She ended the evening in prayer and for the first time I heard a request which was to be repeated in her prayers nearly every day: "Father, let that great day soon come when Your Son comes on the clouds of heaven."

"It will not be long before the Lord Jesus returns," she said. "I want to be here when it happens. In the meantime, there is much work to be done."

As I climbed the stairs to my little bedroom on the third floor that night, it seemed to me that Corrie had not been at all spoiled by the large sphere of influence and fame that was hers. She always had time for everyone. And her burning desire was to tell of God's love, using every opportunity to do so.

On the other hand, I also felt a growing tension between Corrie's relaxed manner and the sense of urgency that I felt. At the beginning of each morning, I would get out my "things to do" notepad and quickly pencil in twenty things that seemed to vie for top priority. Corrie appeared to be tolerant of my lists—it was just that she did not always seem to pay much attention to them.

One afternoon, two days before our planned departure, my list of top priorities had doubled in size. I did not see how I could get everything ready in time. Papers needed to be finalized, passports, visas, and tickets needed final checking, suitcases readied, notes gathered for upcoming speeches. We were about to set to work on these items after a full morning of interruptions, when the telephone rang yet again.

When I answered, I was surprised at the edge of coldness in my voice. It was a young man wanting Corrie's advice on the future direction of his life. He needed to see her "right away." I muffled the mouthpiece and delivered the brief message, expecting—hoping—that she would decline.

Without a second thought, she replied, "Tell him he is welcome to come for a little while this evening."

After giving the boy her message and hanging up the receiver, I protested to Tante Corrie. "There simply is not enough time to receive anybody else. Apart from everything that is still unfinished, we need some rest and privacy."

Firmly, patiently, she looked at me. "God has sent this young man, and we will receive him. Child, you have to learn to see things in the right proportions. Learn to see great things great and small things small.

"When you stand at the gate of eternity, as I did in concentration camp, you see things from a different perspective than when you think you may live for a long time. Every time I saw smoke pouring from the chimneys of the crematorium I asked myself, 'When will it be my turn to be killed or to die?' And when you live like that every day, in the shadow of the crematorium, there are very few things that are really important—or only one—to share with as many people who will listen about the Lord Jesus Christ who is willing that anyone who wants to can come to Him."

And straightaway she prayed, "Lord, I pray that You will help Pam to see things as You see them, that her life will become more relaxed, so that more people will come to know You, Lord. Hallelujah! Amen."

I wondered if it would ever be possible for me to see things as simply as she did. I continued my work, stopping to receive our young visitor that evening. And I had to admit that, although people continued to stream through the house, everything that had to be accomplished somehow did get done. It seemed so odd that I, a young person, had to learn how to be as flexible as this woman fifty years my senior.

Of course there were still many things to learn about Corrie, from the small details to the very important details. Without Ellen's continued hard work behind the scenes, and her coaching me, I would have felt completely unprepared. For example, she taught me the kinds of things that would make Tante Corrie's rigorous life easier: her favorite food, where to order airline tickets, how to shield her from a constant stream of people—and to remember to serve Tante Corrie Dutch rusk with a sugar coating at early morning tea time on her forthcoming birthday just a few weeks away. Birthdays, as I knew, are a very important part of Dutch culture and *beschuit* (rusk) is a tradition.

However, there was one "detail" I almost wished I had not learned.

One evening, after Tante Corrie had retired for the night, Ellen and I were working in the little office on the third floor. I took the opportunity to share my feelings about this new way of life and to ask Ellen about the confines of this type of commitment.

She looked thoughtful, then replied, "Pam, the Bible says that if a grain of wheat does not fall into the ground and die, it remains alone. But if it dies it brings forth much fruit. That is how my life has been with Tante Corrie. If I have been prepared to lay down my life daily and to die to my own desires, it works. If I am not prepared to die to my own desires, it does not work."

"Ellen," I said, "Tante Corrie looks so well, but she is very old. How does she stand up to the long journeys and this exhausting type of life?"

"She loves her work. It rejuvenates her. And she has an amazing capacity to regain her strength after a short rest. She has some problems with her heart, but that is very common in somebody of her age."

The remark about her heart alarmed me.

I lay in bed that night, glad of the thick walls protecting us in the "Agape House" from the heavy rain and penetrating cold of that early April night. Scenes from the previous unusual weeks flashed through my mind—the extraordinary interview with Corrie, the preparations for this taxing journey, and the prayer of my friend who had been impressed with the words *Till death us do part*. Did that really refer to Tante Corrie and me? Judging by her vitality she seemed to have a long time left. Perhaps years. That would mean a life commitment of a very different kind.

Well, I thought, as I lay in bed listening to the rain, these coming months would be a good test. I would see her writing and speaking, handling business and traveling. I would learn how she was first thing in the morning and last thing at night; how she was when she was physically tired and when she was up against spiritual battles. After that, if necessary, I would think about a life commitment. In the meantime I would take each day as it came.

Before falling asleep I thought about my conversation

with Ellen just one hour before. I reflected on her words. Tante Corrie loved her work and needed the total support of her companion; in this position I would have to "die to myself." Those words were to have a deep effect on the next seven years of my life.

3.

A Time to Decide

The very day before our anticipated departure, Tante Corrie awoke with a bad cold. Resisting the temptation to say, "I knew all those visitors were too much for you," I telephoned her doctor. He came immediately to examine her, and left some instructions, including bed rest that day. I accompanied him to the front door. There I learned a little more about Tante Corrie's general state of health.

"She is a strong woman," he began, "and in good health for her age. She has unusual recuperative powers. You should know, though"—he paused with a cautionary glance—"that her heart is not strong. I have advised her to have one full day of bed rest each week." He continued the instructions, warning me to keep her from walking airports, but to get her into a wheelchair. It was also important for her to have two days to acclimatize at each new area before she began speaking.

When he left, I decided I needed to do some research. Not being a nurse, how would I recognize any important symptoms should Corrie develop heart problems on the trip—and what would I do? I decided to do a little reading in a medical book when I got the chance, and the opportunity came later that day. The subject I was looking for was listed under "cardiovascular disease." Much of what I read was too technical for me to really understand but I came away with a little elementary knowledge. According to the book, I should watch for a gray face, bluish lips, and breathlessness, and also in the event of hardening of the arteries or stroke, symptoms such as confusion, forgetfulness, depression, and loss of muscle power.

When Tante Corrie's cold did not improve that day, I was mentally prepared to cancel all travel arrangements. The next morning, however, when I entered her bedroom, I found her busily placing last-minute items in her suitcase.

"Tante Corrie, how are you feeling? Do you intend that we leave today?"

"Oh, yes, child," she said, looking up. "The Lord gave me such blessed sleep. He has touched my body and made my cold better. When the Lord does it, He does a thorough job."

She was indeed completely better. Before I could remark, she asked, "Have you packed *The Hiding Place*s?"

"What do you mean, Tante Corrie?"

"We must have as many copies of my book as we can carry. You know, sometimes, many years ago, when Betsie and I came out of the railway station here in Haarlem we would be moved at the sight of hundreds of people streaming in to catch the next train. She and I would say to each other, 'Wouldn't it be wonderful if we could reach all these people with the Gospel?' And now I *can*. I can reach many more people than that with the Gospel. I want to give a copy of the book to everyone God puts in our path."

And truly, Corrie seemed to use every opportunity, every chance meeting, to share the love of God. I was ever amazed at her boldness.

Our departure was to be from the Amsterdam International Airport, and Ellen accompanied us there. One of the first things she did was to procure a wheelchair for Tante Corrie. "Otherwise," she explained, "Tante Corrie has to walk long distances through the many airports you will visit. Always be sure you have ordered a wheelchair ahead of time to save her extra physical strain. At first it was hard for Tante Corrie to get into a wheelchair, but now I think she rather enjoys it."

We helped Tante Corrie into it. She straightened her coat over her knees and moved her feet to one side so that we could place the hand baggage on the footrest; then she looked up at us with a twinkle in her eyes as if to say, "We are off!" I could not help thinking that it must indeed have been hard for Tante Corrie at first, but I admired the fact that for the sake of the ongoing work, she who was so vigorous was willing to be pushed through the airport corridors.

We said goodbye to Ellen and to Holland, passed through the check-in counter and passport control, and made our way toward the waiting jet a good distance away. Tante Corrie's wheelchair was now pushed by a uniformed airline official. When we reached the door to the airplane, the poor man looked extremely surprised when his very elderly passenger stood straight up and made her way to her seat with a vigor, determination, and speed uncharacteristic of her age.

We settled into our seats in the aircraft and, thinking about the doctor's remarks on the condition of her heart, still in awe of her and not yet knowing her very well, I thought I would venture a question.

"Tante Corrie, is it really necessary to walk so quickly? I think that KLM employee who was pushing you wondered whether you really needed a wheelchair when he saw you getting on the plane."

"All right, child," said Tante Corrie. The matter was quickly dismissed as we prepared for takeoff.

If I thought we were going to relax during the flight, I was mistaken. Even before I stowed our carry-on luggage in the overhead cabinets, she asked me to get out several copies of *The Hiding Place*. On the flyleaf of the first, she wrote: "To my pilot, thank you for giving me such a good flight, Corrie ten Boom, Ps. 91:1." She gave it to the stewardess to pass on to the flight captain, and also gave the girl her own signed copy.

Throughout the flight, she kept up a steady pace of work and lighthearted dialogue, some of which concerned me and my personal life. I realized that Corrie ten Boom cared a lot about the people who worked with her. My well-being was important to her. I felt welcome in her world, and needed, and loved.

On arrival at the airport, Tante Corrie's nephew, Peter, met us and took us to a Geneva hotel. Our room was simple and comfortable, but the thing that struck me first about it was that it contained a double bed. Just one. To Tante Corrie this was obviously all in a day's work. She prepared herself for the night and climbed into the bed completely unembarrassed, falling asleep very quickly. Sleep did not come so quickly to me. I lay as quietly as possible, afraid that any movement might wake her.

The next morning I discovered that the doctor's request that she have two days of rest before doing anything strenuous apparently did not apply to her writing. Tante Corrie was awake and dressed early. After breakfast in our room, she set right to work. Using the double bed and the table as work surfaces, she unpacked from one of the bags all the material relating to her book—notes, typed pages, and notebooks. Her nephew arrived to find Tante Corrie ready for a working session of several hours. The travel had not slowed her one bit, and every available moment was spent researching and planning. I could not but be awed at her energy.

On our second day, Tante Corrie was scheduled to speak at a ladies' meeting. Her preparations for this were as thorough as her previous day's work had been intense. Earnestly, she prayed, "Lord, let every word be from You.

Let me say every word that You want spoken and keep me from saying anything that You do not want to be said."

In her convictions and the pace of her work, I was beginning to sense one thing: Not only did her work take top priority, but for Corrie, time was of the essence.

Then, she surprised me with a request.

"Pam, there are four basic parts to my message. You must help me to be sure that they are included every time I speak."

"What are they, Tante Corrie?"

"I must tell the people that they can come to the Lord Jesus just as they are. Also they must know about the need to forgive their enemies. Then I want to include the fact that the Lord Jesus is coming very soon, and that in the meantime they must live as rich as they are in Him."

To Tante Corrie, she had narrowed her message down to the essentials. But I could not help venturing an opinion. "That is a lot for a one-hour talk, Tante Corrie."

She merely smiled and went on. "Tell me if people are seeing too much of me. Corrie ten Boom must be *behind* the cross."

With her final requests, she surprised and delighted me. "I'd like it if you will wear your red dress," she said. "I want to be proud of my daughter. And will you sit in the front row where I can see you? Please pray for me as I speak."

Preparations completed, her nephew came to collect us. As we drove to an elegant hotel not far from the lovely Lake Geneva, I noticed that Tante Corrie was not looking her best; her face was as gray as the temperamental spring sky.

The room, large and gracious, was full of ladies whom Tante Corrie greeted with loving enthusiasm. Most of them were the wives of foreign diplomats in Geneva, well-dressed, many with long, painted fingernails and fashionable hairstyles. For some reason the atmosphere seemed a bit artificial.

It did not look very promising to me. Not only that, it was all rather threatening. My red dress felt conspicuously simple.

I sat down a bit awkwardly in the front row and the meeting began. At once I noticed one elegant lady in pink, also in the front row, who appeared to be regarding the elderly speaker with some amusement. A sudden flush of indignation ran through me. If only she knew what it cost an old woman to stand for an hour to talk to her.

"When the worst happens in the life of a child of God— and it did—the best remains, and the *very best* is yet to be," Tante Corrie began. From her bag, she slipped out a piece of cloth. I recognized it as the shiny blue cloth I had mistaken for embroidery. She held it up backward, so we were staring at the tangled, knotted, yellow threads of the wrong side.

The lady in pink, who was sitting very near to Tante Corrie, leaned forward to help her turn it to what she thought was the correct side. Tante Corrie, smiling at her, lifted the cloth a little higher so that it was out of her reach and said:

> "My life is like a weaving
> Between my God and me
> I do not choose the colors
> He worketh steadily.
>
> Sometimes He weaveth sorrow
> And I in foolish pride
> Forget He sees the upper
> And I the underside."

As she spoke the last two lines, Tante Corrie turned the cloth around so that instead of tangled threads, we saw a golden crown. And she continued:

> "Not 'till the loom is silent
> And the shuttles cease to fly
> Will God unroll the canvas
> And explain the reason why

The dark threads are as needful
In the skillful Weaver's hand
As the threads of gold and silver
In the pattern He has planned."

She moved immediately into her message. "Do you know Jesus Christ? I don't mean do you know about Him, but do you know Him? I was five years old when I asked the Lord Jesus to come into my heart and He came and He has never let me down. I have talked about Him for nearly eighty years in sixty-four countries of the world where I have traveled, and I have never met anybody who was sorry that they asked Jesus into their heart.

"In my hand I have this book," she went on, lifting her small, black New Testament. "This book has to lie somewhere—in my hand, in my bag, on the table, but it must rest somewhere, and it is the same with your sin. If you do not know Jesus Christ you are carrying your sin, and that is right, because you did it. But there was a moment in the world's history when God took your sin and mine and laid it on Jesus Christ. He has borne your sin. Will you accept Him as your Savior and Lord? You may think you are too bad to come to Jesus. There is only one person who cannot come to Him and that is the person who thinks that he or she is too good to come. I invite you to come to Him."

Since our chairs were arranged in curved rows, I was able to see a good part of the audience from where I sat. Now I could see emotions reflected on the faces of these influential, privileged women—wistfulness, longing, even tears, as she talked about knowing the love of God and His forgiveness. Even the lady in the pink dress was watching intently now. Although I had felt put-off and slightly critical, I was suddenly aware that somehow Corrie had known of these hidden feelings from the moment we had entered the room.

Just as Tante Corrie was finishing her final point, about living as rich as we are in Jesus Christ, there came a very awkward moment. Suddenly she could not find a word. The room was deafeningly silent as Corrie searched for the rest of a sentence that would not come to her. I prayed hard. I glanced around the room, but nobody else seemed perturbed. And then Tante Corrie was back on track in her talk and obviously enjoying it.

Into my mind flickered the notes I had read in the medical book . . . *confusion and forgetfulness* . . . *hardening of the arteries*. Perhaps I am just overreacting, I scolded myself.

The meeting ended, and several of the ladies hurried to the podium to speak to Tante Corrie. First in line was the lady in the pink dress. Silently, I asked forgiveness for my critical thoughts of her.

Back at the hotel room, Tante Corrie went straight to bed. Spiritually she was refreshed, but I could see that physically she was taxed.

Two days after her talk in Geneva, we left for the U.S.A. The flight was to New York with a connection to Miami later the same day. I had remembered to order the wheelchair and it was waiting at the ticket counter. Tante Corrie settled her ample frame into it, and, after the necessary formalities, an employee of Swissair pushed her toward the jumbo jet bound for New York. I glanced at Tante Corrie and thought she looked tired. Her face still had a grayish tinge. At the steps of the aircraft here, in contrast to her vigor at Amsterdam a few days previously, she eased herself carefully out of the wheelchair and slowly mounted the steps of the aircraft, leaning heavily on the strong arm of her aide.

It must be her heart, I thought, *just as we are leaving European soil. I wonder what will happen now.*

We installed ourselves in our seats, Tante Corrie leaned back, and I ventured a question: "Tante Corrie, are you feeling all right?"

With a mischievous look, she replied. "Yes, didn't I play my role well?"

I had to laugh as I fastened my seat belt. In Amsterdam I had asked her to walk a little more slowly and here she was, simply having some fun with me. I relaxed and determined not to be a bothersome nag.

As we flew over the Alps toward America, Corrie began to tell me about the period of time that followed the story told in *The Hiding Place*. I realized it was a part of her life that few people knew about.

The Americans, she said, were kind to her after the war. In the 1940s she had arrived in New York, knowing nobody. It was very lonely. She would choose a street and walk down it. Whenever she saw a church building she knocked at the door and asked if she could give her testimony. At first very few people wanted to listen, and it was very discouraging. She existed on breakfasts consisting of a cup of coffee, a doughnut, and a glass of orange juice.

"One day I met two girls who asked me to lunch with them. I hesitated, not having any money, but they said, 'We want to buy your lunch. We know that you Europeans have suffered much in the war.' On that day I began to love the Americans. We ate a chicken dinner. I will never forget how good it tasted!"

And so our conversation progressed, and we touched upon areas of finance, for Corrie believed firmly that God would supply all our needs, though in typical Dutch fashion, she was very conservative with expenses. The Tante Corrie I had seen up until now was completely unencumbered by money.

She told me about the time when the Lord made it clear to her that she was not to ask for money. It was something she learned quite early in her traveling ministry.

Once, at a meeting in England, she had given her

testimony and also told about a former concentration camp in Germany that had been converted into an attractive building and was being used as a rehabilitation center for those who needed help after the war. During the talk she mentioned some of the material needs and afterward a lady came to her with a check for a substantial amount of money. As Tante Corrie talked to her she saw that the lady had not responded to the Gospel message she had brought. Tante Corrie told her that it was a good thing to give money for evangelistic work, but that the Lord wanted to have much more than her money, He wanted her to put her whole life into His hands. Tante Corrie then told the lady that it was not right for her to accept her check. As she handed it back she saw a proud look come onto the woman's face and she walked away without replying.

Later that day God told Tante Corrie clearly while she was praying, "From now on you must never ask again for money." She responded to the Lord by telling Him that she would obey Him. She would never again ask for any money even though she needed more than ever before.

On the same day she received two letters. One was from a lady in Switzerland who told her that God had put it on her heart to write to Corrie and to say that from that point on she was never to ask for money. The other letter was from her sister, Nollie, in The Netherlands. She wrote: "When I prayed for your work this morning God made it clear to me that you should not ask anybody for financial support. He will provide everything." Tante Corrie told me that during the years of travel this principle had often been severely tested, but that God had always provided for her.

She also explained to me "Christians Incorporated," her U.S. board of directors whose office was situated in Orange, California. When her work in the U.S. expanded she had set up the board to take care of her many business details and arranging of meetings. Having known about a number of Christian organizations, I was amazed that Corrie had reached her mid-eighties and gained an impressive sphere of influence without being encumbered by a weighty organization. She was basically the one-person pilgrim she had been when she started her international work in the mid-1940s. Constant traveling had no doubt been a great help. She simply had to travel light.

Two hours later, after landing in New York, we met with three representatives of her publisher, Fleming H. Revell. Bill Barbour, the company's president, had a shock of silver-white hair, and an obvious deep love for his elderly client. Tante Corrie produced a small notepad from her purse and went through a long list of questions, thoroughly prepared to cover a large amount of material. Not only was there talk of the book about her father, but of several other books as well. It was my first glimpse of Tante Corrie in the business world. And in keeping with what I had already learned about her, the subject of money was not even raised. She really was free of it.

After a four-hour layover, we were on our way to Florida. So much had happened, I could hardly believe that we had left Holland only the week before. On arrival in Miami we were taken to a hotel and there was, at last, the opportunity for some rest. There, on April 15, she celebrated her eighty-fourth birthday. And I was even able to produce some Dutch rusk with powdered sugar for the occasion, remembering Ellen's advice in Holland.

Again, Corrie's idea of rest meant almost constant work on notes for the talks she was to give. Now I saw, so clearly, that Corrie meant it when she had said, "The work comes first."

A couple of days later, at 3:30 on Easter morning when a maid brought tea to the room, Tante Corrie was awake and ready to start the day. The sunrise service at Marine Stadium started at 5 a.m., and when her turn came to speak she brought a powerful message.

From then on, for the next seven months, we traversed the United States ... Boston, Toronto, San Jose, Los Angeles, San Diego ...

When in California she spent time at the office with her board members, under the able leadership of Bill Butler and his wife, Bettie. A system was worked out whereby the organizers of her large meetings could be informed in advance of the needs of their elderly speaker. In spite of her enthusiasm, I was concerned, for her strength was declining. Still she went on, never missing a meeting, and her enthusiasm was unabated.

Knoxville, Charlotte, Williamsburg. ... During those months of 1976, she and I and the seven pieces of luggage traveled thousands of miles. She was often tired, but always faithful to her calling. For example, there was the day we made a plane change—the first of many—in Atlanta.

Seating herself in the wheelchair, Corrie asked, "Pam, do you have a *Hiding Place* ready?" I dug into the bag and gave one to her.

When the skycap came to wheel her, she spoke with her usual warmth. "I expect you know your way about this airport pretty well, don't you?"

"Yes, ma'am," he replied. "I've worked here for twenty years."

"Do you also know the way to heaven?"

And so it went.

By the time we were halfway through the seven-month marathon, Tante Corrie had seen to it that I was much better equipped to be a fellow tramp for the Lord than I had been at the beginning of the journey. I was now the proud possessor of several new items of clothing, brightly colored ones included. My long straight hairstyle had been cut so that it would be easier to maintain, at her suggestion. It was now shoulder-length and turned under. I had allowed one other change. The American ladies wore more makeup than I had been used to, but I decided to experiment, since the new bright colors of my clothes made my fair skin look even paler. Some blusher and new lipsticks were added to the luggage that trailed us everywhere.

On the one hand I was enjoying this new life tremendously. There was a speed, urgency, and challenge to it, also new places, new people, and new lessons in faith daily. A multitude of details had to be covered and the problem-solving assignments challenged me. I wrote to my parents in southern England, "This is such an adventure. I am enjoying it more than anything I have ever done." This part of it fulfilled my longing for adventure perfectly.

On the other hand it was sometimes very difficult. Once, at Washington's National Airport the person whom we had been told would meet us was delayed. We were very tired and the weather was sultry and humid. Faced with a flight of stairs, Tante Corrie in her wheelchair, no porter for the luggage with which I was surrounded, I was suddenly overwhelmed by a feeling of panic. Happily, her host arrived after a few minutes, but I was upset by the incident, wondering how I could keep up this kind of life.

That evening, after Tante Corrie had gone to bed, I sat in the small guest bedroom that had been assigned to me and decided to talk the matter through with the Lord. I put the light out and began to pour out feelings that I had barely even had time to consider during our hectic pace.

This kind of life was simply too hard, I told Him. Tante Corrie's strong sense of call meant that, whatever happened, the ministry was first. Moreover, her strong personality meant that mine was often overshadowed. Her strong visionary character saw to it that new ideas and plans were thought of daily and had to be worked into an already overcrowded schedule. My "things to do today" list was impossibly long. And then there was the endless stream of people. Tante Corrie's extrovert nature and long experience could handle them better than mine. Often I longed to withdraw to a private place, but there rarely was such a place.

"I am not cut out to be a servant," I went on. "Just look at my attitude this afternoon at the airport.

"Father, three months ago I told Tante Corrie, 'I am willing to help you.' At the same time I was making that commitment to You. Now I feel that I don't want to go on. Forgive me my selfishness and help me."

Into my mind came the verse Ellen had shared with me in Haarlem, "Unless a grain of wheat falls into the ground and dies, it abides alone, but if it does it bears much fruit."

I took a deep breath. Learning to die to my own desires for an easier life was obviously going to take some time, I thought.

If Tante Corrie noticed me withdrawing, she never mentioned it.

And the journey went on ... Des Moines, Knoxville, Chicago, Tulsa; three months, four months. Another hotel near the airport, another airport sign, one more Boeing 727, more chicken and carrots served on a plastic tray, cigarette smoke, weariness. Charlotte, Tulsa, Honolulu, Dallas ...

After five months of traveling came the moment I knew I could not put off any longer. In two months' time we would be back in Holland. Was I going to stay with Tante Corrie through whatever was to be the next phase of her life? She never seemed to doubt that we were going to work together, but I had never stated it to her. Now I simply had to decide.

We were in Orange County, California, again, and it was

late summer. Our accommodation was a hotel near Disneyland. The room was a fairly large one with two double beds, some easy chairs and a table. Carpets and drapes were beige and the smell of stale cigarette smoke hung in the air. All of our rooms had become a blur to me.

One afternoon, Tante Corrie received a guest who seemed glad of the chance to be alone with her and I took the opportunity to go for a walk. After so much sitting in cramped conditions on aircraft, I walked as often as possible, but Anaheim did not really cater to pedestrians. Everything was concrete, heat was rising from the pavement, large cars flashed by.

Ambling, without a sense of purpose, I decided to take the streets going west. I remembered how I told myself before this long journey began that there would be time to decide about a life commitment after I had seen this lady in action. I had now witnessed that action. I was impressed by all I saw—her unyielding hard work, her attitude toward business, her care for me. Thinking of her care for me led me to consider honestly a question I had tried to avoid. If I were to make a life commitment to her it would mean giving myself to somebody whom I would probably have to lose by death perhaps before too long. That would be hurtful. I would rather not go through that. With these things in mind I continued my walk on that hard, hot pavement. I wanted to be willing, but was not.

I cannot say how, or exactly why, but as I walked across a certain crack joining two paving stones, it was as if I received a strength from outside myself, as if I had been helped to step across a line that my own will had drawn. At that moment I knew, and the decision was made. We would be together from then on.

Tante Corrie was waiting for me in the hotel room with some tea and shortbread. Her guest left upon my arrival. It was one of the rather rare times of the day when we were alone together. The tea and cookies were tasty. Instead of the staleness, I now felt that there was something cozy even about that hotel room. Once again we were enjoying the atmosphere that the Dutch call *gezellig*. Togetherness.

"Tante Corrie," I offered at one point, "I am going to be sure that I have some good walking shoes for the next time we are back in the States."

I could have been mistaken, but as Tante Corrie looked at me from her discerning eyes, it seemed that they looked more blue and radiant than usual.

Our conversation went on, and tired though she was, Tante Corrie began laying out more plans.

"Wouldn't it be wonderful if my messages could be put on film—that way thousands of people could see them? California is the place where movies are made. Perhaps the Lord will give us a home there. I can envisage the day when it will no longer be necessary to travel."

I merely smiled. How she loved to plan!

Shortly before we flew back to Holland, an unusual incident occurred.

One morning, as usual, I took tea to Tante Corrie's room early. She was awake and her mood was quiet, reflective.

"I've had that dream again."

"What dream is that, Tante Corrie?"

"In my dream I am inside a room from which I cannot escape. I am permanently there and it is rather like a prison. While I am there my message is still going out to the people through films and books and television." I paused. It was not the first time during our trip that she had had this very same dream.

Dreams had been significant in the way God guided the Ten Booms as a family. But it seemed odd to me. There was nothing about her present circumstances that confined her at all. And she was brimming with new possibilities.

There was little time to consider what the dream could mean.

In a few days, we were on our way home to Holland.

It was not until much later that I remembered that dream.

4.

Home

A few weeks after our return to Holland, winter set in. The cold was penetrating. Tante Corrie's work and unceasing stream of visitors continued as usual. What was rather unusual was that she talked increasingly about a home in the United States. She seemed convinced, in her inimitable way, that the timing for this was suddenly right. I marveled at the extraordinary sensitivity she appeared to have when it came to knowing God's plans.

As if to underscore Corrie's yieldedness to God, a letter arrived in the mail one day from an old friend in India. She wrote: "There is one small incident in your life that you probably will not remember, and it is not written in any of your books. But it is what I remember you by more than anything else. You had just arrived to stay with us, and I met you and took you to our guest room. A missionary friend had brought you by car and you had been having a very heavy program through the previous weeks. So you looked around your room and made some remark about how peaceful it was. Then you looked at the friend who had brought you and you said, 'I wish . . .' But you did not finish the sentence. Instead you looked up and said, 'Father, You do all things well. Thank you.' I believe that what you began to say was, 'I wish I could stay longer here,' but that quick turning from your natural wish to thank your heavenly Father for His planning has blessed me often through the years since."

What this said to me was that others had detected Tante

Corrie's sensitivity to the combination of yieldedness and timing. It also said to me that her spirit was probably right in that it was time for her to be given the desire of her heart: a place of her own in America.

We had been back in Holland for about a month when a friend came to visit her one afternoon. I showed him into the long sitting room with its dark green carpet where Tante Corrie was waiting for him in her beige chair, and went to get some refreshments from the little kitchen at the back of the house. As I brought the tray in to them, I could not help overhearing her conversation, and it was on the subject of plans.

"I love making plans," she said, "Even when I was a young girl I made lots of plans. Friends used to ask me how many plans I had and in answer to one of them once I said, 'Sixteen.' 'Huh, how many of those do you think you can work out?' my friend said. I answered her with another question, 'How many plans have you?' 'None,' she replied. 'Well, if I work out only two of my plans I will have done more than nothing.' "

Sure enough, that evening, when the guest had left, Tante Corrie and I had a long talk. We had built a fire and it was cozy in the sitting room.

"Child," said Tante Corrie, and went straight to the point. "I believe that the time has come that the Lord is going to give us a home in the United States. I am a Dutchwoman in heart and soul and will never change my nationality because when I was young and in the Girl Scouts I promised allegiance to the queen. But in America I have so many opportunities that I do not have here in Holland."

"You mean in speaking, Tante Corrie?"

"Yes, but I believe that if I could make short films of my messages they will eventually reach far more people than I could ever reach personally. California is the place to make films."

"And you could do a lot more writing, too."

"Yes, wouldn't it be wonderful to be able to have dictionaries and concordances always ready at hand? They are far too heavy to travel with. In a home of my own it would be much easier. And," she added with a sparkle in her eye, "I have a new goal—to make five films and to complete five books from the house the Lord is going to give us."

We discussed the matter for some time. Orange County, California, was where the headquarters of her board of directors was situated. It would be so much easier for her to be near them. Tante Corrie finished our conversation in prayer to the Lord, asking Him for the right house.

As we got ready for the night I felt mixed emotions. The plan for a house was now definite. It was indeed best for Tante Corrie, and that was very good. But it sounded very confining. Travel, hard though it often was for me, was exciting. The very forward movement of it made me feel that I was getting somewhere. Whatever would it be like when the traveling stopped?

In January, 1977, after only three months in Holland, we once again boarded a plane heading for New York.

I had the habit of using some of the long flight hours to read as many as possible of Tante Corrie's books. They taught me a lot about her and the previous thirty years. On this flight I was reading *Tramp for the Lord* and in chapter eight came across the description of a rather strange incident.

She had traveled to Switzerland for a speaking engagement, but, upon arriving at a certain railway station, she suddenly did not know the names of any of her contacts or where she was supposed to speak. It sounded like a frightening experience, but caught up in the momentum of the book's account of her traveling adventures I nearly passed over it. Only for a moment did I relate the incident to the possibility that she had described symptoms of an illness.

Had she, without knowing, described a small stroke? Glancing at Corrie, I dismissed the thought. There was a relief, a joy, and an infectious lightheartedness about her—she was off on a new adventure.

On arrival at John F. Kennedy Airport we passed through customs more quickly than usual because we had shortly beforehand been issued with green cards that gave us resident alien status in the United States. Visitors' visas could be obtained for only a limited amount of time, necessitating returns to Holland for reentry application. That would now no longer be necessary.

At the airport, any residual doubts about Tante Corrie's buoyancy and mental sharpness were erased. Inside the terminal, we were buffeted by a crush and a rush of people, and tempers seemed to be short. With Tante Corrie safely installed in her wheelchair, I was struggling with the seven pieces of luggage and looking for some help. A porter made it clear to me that although he was willing to push her wheelchair I need not expect any further assistance from him.

"Tante Corrie," I said to her in Dutch, almost in disbelief, "did you hear how incredibly rude that man was?"

"Child," came the answer, also in Dutch, "just be glad you are not married to him."

And as I tried to find another porter I could hear her talking to him: "Say, this is a large airport. Do you know your way all around it?"

I had to smile, knowing so well where that conversation would lead.

Our airline tickets showed our final destination to be Los Angeles, but Tante Corrie had planned a working stopover of several weeks in Florida so that she could do some more work on the book she was writing. It was a very welcome respite. The months in Holland had been busy and I knew there was another period of intense work coming up in the search for a house in California. In Florida we stayed with some friends whose home was located near a bayou on the Gulf of Mexico.

The evening of our arrival, I felt an urgency to be alone. Leaving Tante Corrie in the good hands of our hostess, I put on my walking shoes and decided to do a little exploring. The air was heavy, warm, and relaxing. The flowers and shrubs were glorious, the trees hung in Spanish moss. For once there was not the press of people. Again, I spilled my feelings.

"Lord, I know that a change has to come. Tante Corrie's old body cannot take this strenuous traveling for much longer. But traveling is her way of life. She has done it continuously for thirty-three years. She has had no real 'roots.' Lord, will you please confirm to my heart, apart from hers, that it is Your plan to give her a home, and that she will be happy there?"

Making my way back to our hosts' home I found that a letter had been forwarded there for me. I opened and read it at once. A text that the writer quoted stood out for me:

"I will give back her vineyards to her, and transform her Valley of Troubles into a Door of Hope. She will respond to me there, singing with joy as in days long ago in her youth . . ." (Hos. 2:15, Living Bible).

In my heart I sensed that God had arranged to have me read that verse at that very moment, but I was not clear as to what it meant. The prophet talked about vineyards, singing, and a door of hope and opportunity—but made no specific mention of a home. It was a puzzle, but I was learning to take things I did not understand and put them, as it were, on a shelf in my mind to await further explanation.

The next day we left Florida for California and were met at Los Angeles Airport by the executive officer of Tante Corrie's board. She had her usual happy exchange with the porter, we collected the seven suitcases, and were taken to the same hotel near Disneyland, where, several months earlier, I had made the decision to become Tante Corrie's permanent companion.

Waiting for me was another letter. The writer was unassociated with the person who had written to me in Florida. But I was astounded to read exactly the same verse: Hosea 2:15. Excitedly I took my Bible and reread the words: "I will give back her vineyards to her . . . as in days long ago in her youth. . . ." Now I was even more sure that God must be speaking to me through that verse, and was curious to watch its application to the unfolding future.

After a good night's sleep we began a plan of campaign, first taking a map of the area and pinpointing where we were in Anaheim, forty miles south of Los Angeles. We pulled the easy chairs together and bent over the map. Five miles to the east was Orange, where Corrie's board was located.

Fifty miles to the northeast was the place where World Wide Pictures, producers of "The Hiding Place" movie, had their studio. She had said that she hoped to make some teaching films with them.

"Here is the Pacific Ocean," I said, indicating some cities fifteen and twenty miles to the south. I was getting enthused, for I loved the idea of being near the Pacific Ocean. Whenever I had seen it in atlases in my childhood it had fascinated me.

"Well, Tante Corrie, where shall we start looking, and what kind of house are you thinking about?"

"I would very much like it to be on the ocean," she replied, "but it must be a simple house."

"Do you want to buy it or rent it, Tante Corrie?"

"We will let the board decide that."

"Let's have lots of flowers, Tante Corrie!"

"Ja!"

"Hummingbirds too!"

"Ja!"

52

I found, to my surprise, that my own attitude toward settling in one place was slowly warming.

"Is there anything else you have in mind for this house?"

"It must be all on one level," she said, "I want to be able to receive handicapped people and they will need to be able to get through the doors easily."

We had no inkling that the fact that there were to be no steps would mean much more to her personally in the future than it could ever mean to her guests.

A summary of Tante Corrie's desires for a house were passed on to her board, and shortly afterward we found ourselves in a real estate agent's car heading toward the beach where we were shown a modest home. The view was beautiful but when Tante Corrie heard the price being asked she gave a little shrug of her shoulders and returned to the car. A home at the beach, if this was the average price being asked, was out of the question.

We traveled many miles that day and the sun shone relentlessly. It was an unusually hot February according to the local residents. Heat was rising from the tarmac creating a haze, and it was very tiring. We viewed several possibilities offered by the real estate man but could find nothing suitable. If the price was right, the location was wrong. If the layout looked suitable, there were too many steps.

The next day we tried again, and for several days after that with no success. We were discouraged, and it was suddenly very easy to doubt the promises I had read in Hosea.

One evening we were having dinner with some friends of Tante Corrie in the nearby town of Placentia. They had very kindly prepared a special meal for her and had spared no trouble. The table was handsomely set with a beautiful flower-patterned dinner service and crystal.

During the meal her hostess said: "We would like you to

think about something. Recently we bought a house here in Placentia. Its previous owners have not yet moved out, but will do so at the end of this month. Perhaps it would be suitable for your needs, Tante Corrie?"

She went on to describe the house, and again the fire of excitement kindled within me. Her description fit exactly the guidelines Tante Corrie had laid down.

We drove past the house on our way back to the hotel late that night. During the journey her friends told Tante Corrie that she could rent if from them for as short or as long a period as she desired. Slowing at the curb, all we could see was a dark shadow outline of a house. No matter, for Tante Corrie was sure that it was the right one. When we got back to our room at the hotel she literally danced for joy. Taking me by the waist, she swung me around, singing, *"Wij hebben een huis, wij hebben een huis!"* ("We've got a house!")

The next day one of the owners drove with us to view the house in Placentia, which I learned means "a pleasant place" in Spanish. The first thing that I noticed about the town when I saw it in daylight was that it was full of trees—palms, conifers, eucalyptus, and birch, which pleased me. The second impression was less enthusiastic: It was the middle of suburbia. There was mile after mile of very similar houses.

The house was situated in a middle-class neighborhood, a mile from the stores, on a side street, the middle of three houses on a short block. The previous owners were still occupying the house and were not home so on that first visit we viewed it from the outside only. I was rather disappointed.

It was a rather nondescript low house—a double garage on the left, to the right a cream-colored iron gate that enclosed the walkway to the front door. All that could really be seen of the house was a wing containing a large window. The front of it had cream-colored wooden slats and the roof was of dark brown, wooden shakes.

The front yard contained a couple of conifers and some juniper bushes. To the left of the garage was a wooden gate with a couple of chinks through which we peered and had a limited view of what was described to us as "a low-maintenance yard." The back lawn was bordered by a flower bed on two sides. Plastic had been placed over the earth in the flower beds and covered with small pieces of red volcanic rock. It looked very bare—not very attractive to humming-birds. There were a couple of small fir trees and one beautiful Norfolk Island Pine in the left-hand corner. Covering the whole of the right-hand side of the yard was a children's play area full of sand, and a swingset.

"I hope you don't mind if I turn this into a garden?" ventured Tante Corrie. The owner had no objection to her doing whatever she liked either inside or out to make this house into a home where she would be happy and comfortable.

A few days later, the previous occupants having moved out, Tante Corrie and I had our first chance to see the house's interior. From the hall just inside the front door we could view the whole living area. The low ceilings made the rooms rather dark. In front of us was the sitting room that had large sliding glass doors through which we could see the yard. To our left, partly divided from the sitting room by a brick wall with a fireplace, was the dining room. Beyond was the kitchen, which appeared more light and green. It had bright yellow-flowered wallpaper and a gray-and-white tiled floor. It was the only cheery room I had seen so far. The darkness was caused by the thick, dark wood and a patio that ran the length of the back of the house.

The other rooms had dull gold-colored wallpaper and the carpet was avocado green shag. Walking down the hall, we found ourselves in another corridor from which led four bedrooms. The master bedroom at the front of the house was large and airy with a picture window facing the street, its own bathroom and small dressing room. At the opposite end of the corridor was the room that we decided was the most suitable for me. In between were two smaller bedrooms, which would be a guest room and an office. I was amused by the plentiful closet and cupboard space. I wondered what we were going to put in them. All we owned was in our suitcases.

Tante Corrie walked back to the sitting room and looked through the sliding doors out into the very unimaginative garden.

"This is where we will put my desk, looking toward the outside," she said, indicating a space in front of the glass door. Her eyes were bright and I suspected she was already envisioning the flowers.

Then she said, "When I stepped into this house the Lord said to me, 'From this place you will reach more people than you have reached in your whole life up until now.' That is a lot. I do not know how He will do it, but He will."

On February 28, 1977, two months after our departure from Holland we moved in. I also noted that it was thirty-three years to the day since Corrie's arrest and the beginning of her imprisonment in 1944.

"We are going to call this 'Shalom House.' The Lord will give His peace here," she declared. I, too, felt the peace of this place. Yet I wondered how Corrie could be so certain that this was to be her home base from now on. My answer came immediately.

Some items of borrowed furniture had been brought for her use until she was settled with her own furniture, but the thing that caught our eye on the first day of residence was that the house was full of plants, a gift from a local church. They had borrowed a key from the owners of the house and it was a complete surprise for Tante Corrie. The man responsible for placing the plants in the house was the owner of a nursery and he came by later in the day to check on them and to ask Tante Corrie which plants she would like for the garden. Without hesitation she asked for some orange trees.

"I will bring you some in a few days and some bougainvillaea bushes. And what I would really like to do, to cover the dark wood of the back patio, is to bring you some vines."

As he said it there was an immediate connection in my mind with the words from Hosea, "I will give back her vineyards to her. . . ."

True to his word, the nurseryman returned before the end of the week, his pickup truck loaded with shrubs, small trees and bushes. We led him to the back garden and Tante Corrie superintended the planting herself.

Chopping through the caked, cracked, and tired-looking earth, it was with difficulty that the nurseryman dug holes and planted the citrus trees in the places Tante Corrie indicated. Between them he placed smaller shrubs and some rose bushes. Directly opposite the glass door from the sitting room where she wanted to have her desk he placed a baby orange tree, a special gift to Tante Corrie.

Two very small plants were embedded next to the vertical beams supporting the patio. They were the promised vines.

Next from the pickup truck appeared several bougainvillaea bushes, though they were not recognizable as such then. A couple went in the backyard, and the others were planted in front so they would eventually cover the iron railings outside Tante Corrie's bedroom window.

These small plants were more than love gifts; they seemed like the promise of new life and hope in the weary soil. I would one day be thankful for these trees and flowers in a way I could not imagine then. The next step was to improve "Shalom House's" interior. The somber wallpaper was stripped off and the walls painted off-white. We left the cheerful kitchen wallpaper where it was and Tante Corrie's bedroom with its cream walls was light enough so we made no changes there.

Accompanied by a new friend who knew the local stores, I went on several shopping expeditions. Among other things we bought a Queen Anne style oval table with six matching chairs in glowing dark red cherry wood, a white semicircular sofa, and three beds. The headboard we chose for Tante Corrie's bed was of carved, dark wood and had a matching bedside table. A bedspread with a green fern pattern on a white background matched the green of the curtains and carpet. There was a reclining chair for the corner of her room and a square table next to the window. A television set and bookcase completed the furnishing of Tante Corrie's bedroom. In the sitting room we placed a large desk overlooking the garden, with a direct view of the vines and citrus trees, and easy chairs on each side of the fireplace. The white sofa, with a coffee table in front of it, covered part of two walls. Shalom House was beginning to look like home. I was particularly pleased with the oval table. It was a lovely piece of furniture, reminiscent of the table around which her family used to gather every day in the Beje in Haarlem.

Tante Corrie's joy knew no bounds. "It is so wonderful to sleep with my head on the same pillow every night. I have not been so happy since the days when I lived with my family in the Beje."

Another fragment of the Hosea passage flickered through my head: ". . . singing with joy as in days long ago in her youth. . . ."

She sent to Holland for some small items, for the notebooks that she had accumulated through the years, and for her music.

The house, though equipped with larger items of

furniture, was by no means complete. The owners of the house, keen to help Tante Corrie get established, had informed several neighboring churches of her presence in their area. The result was that over the next few weeks she was the guest at several "showers." There were bedroom, kitchen, bathroom, and patio showers. She enjoyed herself immensely.

"Pam," she said, "Showers are real American. Ellen and I were asked to go to a 'baby shower' once and we had never heard of it. We went to a store and asked if they could give us a little 'shower' suitable for a baby. Later we learned that it means a shower of gifts. How generous the American people are."

Soon, as a result of the shower gifts to her, Tante Corrie's home was furnished with all necessities, and more. She spoke to the people whenever a shower was held.

"Some people think that Corrie ten Boom is going to retire. That is not so—the Lord is giving me new tires."

As soon as possible we removed the swingset, filled the sandbox with good topsoil and planted a rose garden. Friends gave Tante Corrie some birdfeeders, a birdbath, and a hummingbird feeder. Each day, before she started her work, she checked the garden, walking from one end to the other, making sure that the birdfeeders were full of seed and nectar. Although we waited hopefully, there was no sign yet of a hummingbird.

One day a minister from Santa Ana, ten miles to the south, telephoned.

"We have heard that Corrie ten Boom has come to live in Orange County and we wonder if there is anything we can do for her. Does she need anything for her new home?"

"Pastor, thank you very much, but we can really say that all needs have been provided. There is one item we do not have and hope to buy one day and that is a record player. If your people felt so led, perhaps they might like to make a contribution toward one."

A very short time later the pastor called again: "I've got Tante Corrie's record player. When can we come and install it?"

He told us: "When I mentioned to our people Tante Corrie's desire to have a record player we took up a collection and it came to $583.00. I went to a dealer and explained what I was looking for. When he heard who the recipient of the gift was to be, he said, without knowing the amount collected, "I will sell this one to you at cost price to myself if you like it. Turntable, speakers, etc. would come to $550, plus sales tax of $33—that is a total of $583.00."

The pastor excitedly proclaimed that this was the instrument the Lord intended Tante Corrie to have. He brought it at once and installed it. Very soon the music of Bach, Handel, and Vivaldi resounded through the house.

Although she had stopped traveling, Tante Corrie's life remained extremely busy. A large number of people had already crossed Shalom House's threshold. I found myself with mixed feelings as I thought about this new way of life. It was very good that Tante Corrie was so happy in her new home and I was glad for her. On the other hand, although she made sure that I had time away from the house, I found it confining to be restricted to one place. I had lost count of the times I had served tea to guests. "I really am a servant," I thought as I accompanied yet another group of people to the front door. "Am I really cut out for this?"

That same evening, in the sitting room that was so much brighter now with its white walls and sofa and several lamps, Tante Corrie and I had a disagreement.

It was on as silly a subject as doormats. We always talked through any purchases that were to be made, but I had not done so on this occasion and had bought two smart green doormats, rather highly priced I had to admit. Tante Corrie thought they were too expensive and asked me to exchange them for smaller ones. This led to my telling her about the fact that I was not entirely happy in my role.

"Why not, when the Lord has given us such wonderful opportunities to reach so many people?"

There it was again, the work always came first.

"Tante Corrie, I feel overwhelmed by all these people. We never have any private life. I don't love them the way you do. Can't you see that many of them are simply coming here to meet Corrie ten Boom? They are taking valuable time, taxing your strength, and I spend half my life making tea."

"Pam, making tea is such a small thing. And as for time, all our times are in God's hands, even the difficult ones."

I thought about it later after Tante Corrie was in bed. If it was true that all our times are in God's hands, then there could be no possibility of a mistake. Perhaps my being in this confining role in a house many thousands of miles away from home and family was then in His timing.

A couple of months after we had moved in, Tante Corrie added a part-time, nonresident housekeeper to her staff. It was obvious that we needed assistance in running the house. Elizabeth Burson, white-haired and motherly, took over the cooking, shopping, and as many housekeeping duties as possible.

One day a friend offered Tante Corrie the loan of a Hammond organ. We debated where to put it and decided that the dining room was the right place, on the short wall that divided it from the kitchen. It fit exactly, and we hung a light over it so that she would be able to see her music clearly. Nearly every day Tante Corrie played, sometimes Bach or Mendelssohn, sometimes Dutch or English hymns. She sat as straight as she was able on the backless, hard organ stool. The light, directly above her head, made her hair even more silvery. Often, she sang, and I sometimes joined her, singing the melody while she sang the alto part, and each time I heard her singing I remembered the verse from Hosea: ". . . She will respond to me there, singing with joy. . . ."

My mind would also go back to the earlier part of the verse: "I will . . . transform her Valley of Troubles into a Door of Hope." Her whole attitude was full of excitement and hope and there was no doubt that there were very many opportunities for continuing her ministry. I tended not to think about that part of the verse that mentioned the valley of trouble. There was no such valley in her life now.

At intervals during the day Tante Corrie walked out onto the patio, settled herself onto one of the green and blue chaise longues that had been given by another local church, and took a ten-minute nap. I checked on her sometimes from inside the house. Often when she was not sleeping, her hands would be raised in her characteristic prayer gesture. Sometimes she was quietly regarding her garden. Sparrows had found their way to the birdfeeder and she loved watching them.

She continued to supervise as many as possible of the proceedings inside Shalom House.

"Let's have a mantlepiece over the fireplace," she said one day. I looked doubtful. "I don't think Americans have mantlepieces above fireplaces these days, Tante Corrie."

"Never mind, we will have one made," she said and we placed an order with a local carpenter who carried out her instructions. Above it she hung a piece of silk Indonesian batik cloth in a style reminiscent of that seen in Dutch households many decades before. It hung from a rod as a wall hanging does, covering the wall to the mantlepiece, anchored on the mantle and allowed to hang over the ledge. It was unusual but quite attractive and she loved it. She placed on her mantlepiece some framed photographs and several small items given to her on journeys around the world. One day I saw an unusual little object standing on the shelf—a small, broken plastic vial filled with tiny flowers and weeds she had collected from the garden.

"What is that, Tante Corrie?"

"I have put it there as a reminder. Just look at all the beauty around us. We have a garden and I am excited every day to be in it. The friends have even given us orange trees. What a miracle for a Dutch person! Every day I can lie out in the sun and see the wide blue sky. But I remember the day when I was in prison in solitary confinement and a guard came to take me for questioning."

She went on to explain that she had been inside for a long time, and the way to the interrogation room was through an open courtyard. What joy she felt in breathing fresh air and feeling sun on her face.

"I looked down and saw some blades of grass and some shepherd's purse growing between the paving stones. When the guard was not looking I quickly bent down, picked a handful and put them inside my dress. After the interrogation was over, when I was back in my cell, I found an old broken medicine bottle and arranged my flowers in it. I hid it behind my mug on my table so that the guard would not see it through the opening in the cell door. It was my garden, the only beautiful thing in my cell.

"I was so happy with it. I have made this little replica of it so that I can show it to my guests and tell that I can say with Paul when he writes to the Philippians: 'I know what it is to be in need, and I know what it is to have plenty.'"

The day came when the items Tante Corrie had sent for from her Dutch house arrived. Her board had asked her Dutch secretary to maintain the house and she had dispatched the requested items—books, notebooks, music. Tante Corrie also sent to the owner of the Beje watchshop in

Haarlem and asked him to send a small mantle clock. It soon arrived. About eight inches high with a brown outer casing, gold-colored face, Roman numerals, and black hands, it was a friendly little timepiece, and found a home in the center of the mantle.

As often as possible we held our morning devotions together on the patio. The little vines were beginning to grow now, putting out fresh leaves. The roses had foliage, too, and the tiny citrus trees, while they did not seem to be growing yet, looked healthy. Two months after moving in we were sitting quietly together when suddenly there was a strange whirring sound overhead. We looked up and hovering in space, then darting, hovering again, then swooping, flashing green and red with a needle-like beak almost as long as his minute body was the first hummingbird. Tante Corrie looked at me with the delight that I supposed only a European could feel on seeing such a beautiful creature in her own garden.

She was home.

5.

His Strength in Her Weakness

During our first two months in California, Tante Corrie often repeated how the Lord told her when she first crossed the threshold that she was going to reach more people from Shalom House than she had done in her whole life up until then.

How is she going to do it, I thought one morning, as I walked from my room to the kitchen to prepare tea. I glanced outside at the garden, and was once again amazed at the generative power of California sunshine. I was sure that a similar amount of growth on the little vines, for instance, would have taken twice as long in Europe. Tante Corrie's little orange tree was looking healthy but its progress was slow. We could not wait for the appearance of oranges.

Having prepared the tea tray, I made my way to Tante Corrie's bedroom, recalling several things that had taken place already.

First there was the emergence of a new daily pattern. The day always began as this one was, by my entering her room with a sense of expectancy. Early morning was when Tante Corrie loved to make plans. Often I could tell she had been awake for some time. Usually she had drawn back the heavy drapes on the window facing east in order to watch the sunrise. I was always curious as to what the Lord would perhaps have told her on any particular morning.

One thing troubled me a little about her gazing out that window. I could not wait for the bougainvillaeas to become

more established so the railings would not be so obvious;
somehow I sensed that having iron bars outside her window
was reminding her of her prison days. She had told me that
since her traveling had stopped she tended to think more
about the atrocities of the concentration camp, though she
never went into any detail.

Nearly every morning, I would find Tante Corrie lying
in bed holding her beloved copy of J.B. Phillips's paraphrase
of the New Testament with its worn black cover. As I
entered, she would greet me, her face radiant, and she would
share a portion of the Bible with me, reacting as though she
were reading it for the first time. I marveled at her constant
delight in the Lord. Then our day's work began—more
writing, more plans. But that was typical of Tante Corrie.

The other important thing that had happened was the
unusually rapid way we had become surrounded by new
friends.

During the first week at the house Tante Corrie said,
"Let's go and meet the neighbors and take them one of my
books." I was a bit startled at this confident approach until I
realized that there was absolutely no ego involved.

One new and very dear friend was Sharon Lightfoot, a
nurse who lived in one of the houses immediately behind
ours. Her particular sense of humor reminded me of England
and so did her peaches-and-cream complexion. Equally dear
were Grady and Maurine Parrott who lived a few houses
away. They had a very attractive garden that Tante Corrie
and I admired, hoping that one day ours would be similarly
colorful. Maurine was very petite, and when Grady smiled it
was as if the sun came out. There were many other neighbors
whom we wanted to get to know better. I was impressed by
the way they all respected Tante Corrie's privacy, and by
their offers of help.

Often, neighbors did not wait for a visit from us. Two

weeks before, for instance, the doorbell rang, and Tante Corrie led into the house a dark-haired cheerful man who explained that he and his family lived just a couple of blocks away. I was involved in typing some notes for one of Tante Corrie's books. It required a lot of concentration and I was not enthusiastic about the unexpected interruption.

"My wife Jane became a Christian through reading your book *The Hiding Place*, Tante Corrie," he said, "may she come and meet you?"

"Why, of course," was the reply, "come any time you like."

"We want to offer our services to help you in any way we can, Tante Corrie," the man went on.

I had heard that before but although those who offered help were usually sincere, what they did not realize was that if we were to take up all the offers of assistance it would take more administrative time than there was available.

"Thank you very much," returned Tante Corrie.

A few days later his wife Jane arrived with her three children, blonde little Kelly, aged eight, and her two younger brothers. As they came into Shalom House so did the aroma of freshly baked bread. Jane produced from her bag two loaves for Tante Corrie and also fresh vegetables from their garden.

I was quite ashamed of my impatient attitude when her husband had first called on us, and even more so shortly afterward when we asked him to repair the garbage disposal unit. He fixed it with unusual precision, and told us that he was a mathematics professor at the local university. Jane and Vuryl Klassen were the first volunteer helpers, and I thought that only Tante Corrie could have procured a university professor as a handyman.

Stepping now into Tante Corrie's sun-filled bedroom, I saw from the twinkle in her eye as I greeted her that spring morning that she was looking forward to the work ahead of her. Not only was she to have a meeting with her publisher, but there was also to be a board meeting of Christians, Incorporated, that evening.

When publisher Bill Barbour arrived later to discuss forthcoming books, Tante Corrie received him on the patio. They discussed publication dates for her new book, *Each New Day*, a daily devotional. And by the time Bill left, Tante Corrie was fired with new enthusiasm. She was never happier than when she was on the subject of books, and now besides, she knew for certain that *Each New Day* would be published before Christmas that same year, 1977.

Elizabeth, the housekeeper, prepared a light supper, and at 6 p.m. the members of Corrie's board began to arrive. There were ministers, businessmen, a lawyer, each one very able and gifted in his own field and desiring to do whatever he could to help Tante Corrie achieve her goals. Some of the gentlemen were old friends whom she had known since she first began to travel in the United States. Others she had met for the first time only in recent years when her board came into being.

We met around the oval table in the dining room, and talked for two and a half hours after supper. Tante Corrie gave a report of the activities in Shalom House up until now, but seemed especially keen to talk about the growing desire in her heart to help prisoners. Very shortly, filming was to begin on a half-hour film called, "One Way Door" especially for prison inmates, which World Wide Pictures, the filmmaking arm of the Billy Graham Association, was to produce. Again, I gave a fleeting thought to the iron railings outside her window.

At 9:30 p.m. the meeting ended and she was very tired. I was concerned that she get into bed at once, but she did not heed my suggestion.

"Let's talk on the patio," she said, "and make some plans." As Tante Corrie preceded me down the corridor to the sitting room, I was mindful that the little stoop in her shoulders, as I viewed her from my position behind her, underlined her eighty-five years and made her look very vulnerable. Yet again I marveled at her drive.

As I walked past the coffee table I brushed against a little china vase containing yellow and white daisies, causing it to fall and break. I was rather upset about it, because it had been a recent shower gift and looked quite valuable.

"Child," said Corrie, watching me wipe up the spilled water, "don't worry about it. It hasn't got eternal life."

In a moment, we seated ourselves in patio chairs near the hummingbird feeder and the vines.

"Do you know what we must do?" began Tante Corrie. "We must start a prayer meeting especially for prisoners, and ask the Lord to show us ways to help them."

So that was it. I knew she had been preoccupied with prisoners and their needs lately.

"Where can we hold it, Tante Corrie? If we do it here at your house I think we could be overrun by people wanting to meet you."

"What would you think," she said, "if we asked our neighbors Grady and Maurine if they will hold it in their house?"

And so Tante Corrie was busy again, drawing into her projects anyone who would help.

We consulted our neighbors and they readily agreed. At 7:30 p.m. the next Monday we held our first weekly prayer meeting for prisoners. Grady led the meeting and Maurine was the perfect hostess.

When Tante Corrie became preoccupied with a particular need and began to pray about it, it often happened that the opportunity arose for her to become identified personally with the subject of her prayers. It was not surprising, therefore, when shortly after this, an invitation came from the chaplain of San Quentin State Prison for her to speak to the inmates. She readily accepted.

When the time came to visit San Quentin State Prison, several months later, I noted with some interest that work on Tante Corrie's film for prisoners, "One Way Door," was already completed. However, I was concerned about the trip, for several times in recent weeks, Tante Corrie had mentioned an odd feeling in her chest. "I can feel my heart," she said. "It does not hurt, but I can feel it." Her color did not look very good to me, and she was sometimes a bit breathless.

She was tired; I could see it. And during our flight, she talked about prison life and told me that ever since her own imprisonment it was very difficult for her to hear the security gates closing behind her.

"I never forget that I was once a prisoner," she said. "We were never allowed to make a decision, and when I was released and back in Holland it was at first difficult for me to make even the normally easy decision about which train to take if I needed to travel somewhere."

We spent the night in the city of San Francisco and in our time with the Lord the next morning asked Him for strength and health for Tante Corrie to accomplish this mission.

Our driver came, and the drive from San Francisco across the Golden Gate Bridge was spectacular. After several miles, in sharp contrast to the beauty behind us, the formidable prison walls rose up in front of us. Soon we joined the queue of wives, children, friends, and relatives awaiting the strict security check before being allowed to visit in San Quentin. We were all given a stamp on our right hands and Tante Corrie tried to talk to as many of the tired-looking wives and relatives as possible.

"It is such a burden and sorrow they have to carry. How the Lord loves them. How they need Him."

The Protestant chaplain came out to greet Tante Corrie and to take her into the institution. After a very heavy door had closed us in, he led us across a quadrangle to a light and attractive building, the Protestant chapel. Many men were gathered there, black, white, Hispanic, Indian, Oriental, all ages, some tidy and well-groomed, others dirty, many with long hair and beards. Through the chapel door, some of the inmates looked curiously, even condescendingly, at their very old visiting speaker. Before we entered, the chaplain gave us certain rules to keep during the whole time we were inside the prison: "Do not separate from the group. Many of these men are dangerous. They are not here at San Quentin because of talking in Sunday school. I was once held for a while in the chapel with a knife at my throat."

We joined the inmates in the pews, and the friendlier ones introduced themselves. Many had become Christians after being sentenced. The man to my left was very kind and helped me find the place in the hymnbook. Someone said later that he had been convicted for killings of nine people. Some had been there for more than twenty years. When Tante Corrie got up to speak I could almost hear the unspoken thoughts in the minds of the men around us: "What does that old lady think she can say to men like us?"

She made her way slowly to the front, her favorite red dress a bright contrast to the grayness of the prison atmosphere. Reaching the podium, Tante Corrie smiled at the crowd and said: "Boys, I know what it feels like to be behind a door that only opens from the outside . . ." and went on to share her prison experiences. I could feel the atmosphere in the room becoming less tense. The men were listening, for she had touched their deepest pains.

After she had finished speaking, they lined up to talk.

Many expressed their love for her. One man gave her the gift of a postage stamp with "I love you" written on the back.

The very full day at San Quentin seemed like a week to me, concerned as I was about the state of her heart. We caught the plane from San Francisco in the late afternoon, and it was with an inward sigh of relief that I pulled into the garage of Shalom House that evening. Surely she will not be able to undertake many more of this type of assignment, I thought.

After the visit to San Quentin, Tante Corrie did not make a quick return to her previous vigor and a few days later she consulted a heart specialist. After carrying out tests he diagnosed "heart block." Her heart was beating too slowly and he suggested that she consider the insertion of a pacemaker. It was a simple procedure, he explained, whereby a small metal box is placed under the skin just below the right collarbone. A narrow catheter running through a vein leading to the heart transmits electrical impulses so that the heart beats regularly.

It sounded like a simple solution. I hoped so much that Tante Corrie would choose to have the pacemaker. I didn't want her to go to heaven just yet.

Tante Corrie asked me to arrange for members of her board and other friends to come to Shalom House to pray with her. And on a Saturday afternoon in October, a week or so after the San Quentin visit, they gathered around her as she sat in one of the reclining chairs in the sitting room.

"Friends," she said, "it seems that I have a choice. My heart is beating slower and slower; sometimes it goes at only twenty beats per minute. It cannot get much slower than that or I will die. The doctor says that a pacemaker will help me and give my heart a regular rate. My choice is between going to heaven or having a pacemaker. The wonderful thing for me would be to go to heaven, but I will be there for eternity and here I can help to build the kingdom of God through books and films. Pray for me that I will know what to do."

Her friends took oil, anointed her forehead, and prayed. After they had done so, they and I had the certainty that God was going to give her more time on earth to complete her planned work. She accepted it as the will of God, and we made arrangements for her to enter the hospital as soon as possible.

With a friend, I waited in the lobby the day after Tante Corrie's admission and finally the surgeon emerged from the operating room to say that the pacemaker was in place and that Tante Corrie had been taken to intensive care for a few hours. I was permitted to stay with her there and she told me that the procedure had been a very trying ordeal.

"Pam, it was so difficult and painful. I was not given general anesthetic and had to lie absolutely still on the hard operating table for two hours. There were four times when I thought I could not bear it. Then I saw a hand pierced by a nail and I could thank the Lord Jesus for the far worse pain that He suffered for my sins. It made me quiet and thankful."

A few days later I drove Tante Corrie back to her Shalom House and she wrote a letter to her friends: "I am still rather weak, but am enjoying a heart that beats a regular seventy-two beats per minute. My pulse is checked with the doctor's office through the telephone. What wonderful technical ability. Every few weeks my arms will be connected to a little machine that is held against the telephone. In that way my heartbeat is registered from a distance. The Bible says, in Psalm 139, 'You discern my thoughts from afar.' That is important. You and I are in God's 'intensive care' day and night. What peace it gives to know that fact."

In the weeks following the pacemaker operation Tante Corrie was able to carry on her work with a measure of increased strength. We had now been in Shalom House for seven months. It was an indication to me of the tender love of God that He had not allowed this to happen during her traveling days, but at a time when she could take as much rest as she felt she needed.

How I enjoyed the relatively few quiet evenings we were able to spend together in her home. There were more of them than usual in the weeks after the insertion of the pacemaker, and we made the most of them. Whenever possible, we put a complete stop to the day's activities and sat together on the white semicircular sofa with our needlework. She had completed several pieces of cross-stitch embroidery recently, a runner for the coffee table and a few cushion covers. I, too, had made a couple of items.

Often we took turns reading aloud while the other embroidered. A book I particularly enjoyed was about the previous queen of the Netherlands, Princess Wilhelmina. She had been a wise and beloved queen, a Christian, and Tante Corrie had known her personally. She told me about her visits to the Dutch Royal Palace "'t Loo" near Apeldoorn where the two ladies had animated discussions together. She described one particular dinner scene at the palace.

Each of those being served the meal had their own footman behind their chair. Princess Wilhelmina, like her guest, was a lady of strong character and opinion, and I would like to know what the statement was that evoked the reply from Tante Corrie: "Your Highness, I don't agree with you at all!" laying down her napkin very definitely on the table to emphasize her conviction.

Immediately the footman leaned forward and removed her half-finished dinner. Tante Corrie had not known that in palace protocol the laying down of a napkin meant that it was time for the footman to remove the plate. How she laughed as she told the story. I laughed, too, and remembered at the same time that it was because of a vow to this lady that Tante Corrie would not give up her Dutch nationality.

One afternoon during these weeks of recuperation from the pacemaker operation, Tante Corrie came into the office with a look of triumph on her face and a book in her hand.

"A child has been born," she announced, "Let's celebrate!"

The mail delivery had brought the first copy of her latest book *Each New Day*. She, Elizabeth, and I laid down our work. I went to the nearest bakery while Elizabeth put the kettle on and the three of us sat around the oval table and celebrated with coffee and cream cakes. Such was Tante Corrie's flair for living that she could make an occasion of something at very short notice, and this occasion indeed required it. It was a big moment, the birth of her first book written at Shalom House.

And still, she was ever seeking ways to increase her knowledge in order to become more effective in the Lord's service. To improve her writing technique she studied many books, particularly biographies and autobiographies. One was an account of what happened in the lives of a number of people who claimed to have seen the glory of God.

We talked about the book as she lay in her bed one cold evening in January, 1978.

"Child," said Tante Corrie, her young and eager spirit looking through her old blue eyes, "these people I have been reading about saw some of the Lord's glory. I would so much like to see that, too. I am going to ask Him."

At once, she lifted her hands and prayed: "Father, will you show to me, too, something of Your glory? Will You keep us so close to Your heart that we see things as it were more and more from Your point of view?"

As I turned out the light and went to my room, I was sure of at least one thing. God answered Tante Corrie's prayers in extraordinary ways. I knew she would see His glory. Did that mean she would go to heaven soon? While I knew that she would consider it the very best thing for her, I hoped not. I loved her very much and did not want to lose her. Besides, the five books and five films were not yet completed.

Alone in my room, I immersed myself in a book. Near 11:30, I was surprised by the sound of Tante Corrie's footsteps padding down the dark corridor. By that time she was usually long asleep. Her radiant face looked in at my door.

"Are you still awake? The Lord has been talking to me and I want to tell you about it." She came and sat on the bed.

"I asked the Lord if I must die soon."

" 'No, not yet,' was His reply."

"May I still see something of You in this time? I should like it so much to have more joy and that in the films people can read joy in my eyes to Your honor."

"Yes, you will see something of Me."

"Pam also?"

"Yes, but later."

"Do You come soon?"

"Yes, but you come first in heaven. Very shortly after that I will come again."

I was nearly as excited as she was. The Lord seemed to indicate that she would be able to continue for some time in active ministry. How wrong I was. The Lord was, in fact, indicating another kind of ministry, one that I could never have imagined.

Had I known I may have been more tolerant, but I did not know. Life in Shalom House, although exciting and rewarding, could be tiring and irritating, too.

On Elizabeth's day off the next week, when I was especially busy anyway, there were unexpected visitors who took two hours of the valuable time I had hoped to put into typing part of one of her new manuscripts. There was a pile of letters to answer, dinner to be cooked, and I had not even had time to write to my family. This life was simply too demanding and I told Tante Corrie so.

She tried to counsel me: "Pam, live as rich as you are in Jesus Christ. He has plans, not problems for our lives.

"Before she died in the concentration camp my sister Betsie said to me, 'Corrie, your whole life has been a training for the work you are doing here in prison . . . and for the work you will do afterward.'

"The life of a Christian is an education for higher service. No athlete complains when the training is hard. He thinks of the game, or the race," she said, opening her Bible. "Look what Paul wrote. 'In my opinion whatever we may have to go through now is less than nothing compared with the magnificent future God has planned for us.'

"Looking back across the years of my life," said Tante Corrie, "I can see the working of a divine pattern, which is the way of God with His children. Take from the Lord the power He is willing to give you at this difficult time. One day you will see His pattern, too."

I knew she was right in her counsel. Her life had proved it, but it did not provide any immediate answers for me. I felt double-minded; on the one hand thrilled with my privilege of helping her, on the other hand overwhelmed by the requirements of the commitment. Would it ever be possible for me to reach a place of consistent peace in the role of servant? The time was soon coming when I would need every bit of strength.

6.

A Time to Make Haste

At the end of February, 1978, we celebrated the first anniversary of Tante Corrie's move to Shalom House, taking stock of all that she had been enabled to do: One film had been completed, and so had two books. We asked the Lord for strength to complete what still remained of her goal.

I had noticed a difference in Tante Corrie since her prayer the month before when she asked to see something of the glory of the Lord. For one thing, although she used the prayer I had heard her repeat dozens of times—"Father, let that great day soon come when Your Son comes on the clouds of heaven"—she never again talked of being present for the event. She was convinced that she would go to heaven first and would not see Jesus Christ's return.

She seemed to be working with a renewed intensity as if an invisible clock were set at a time that could not be exceeded. We often talked about heaven and she expressed a longing to be there, but she rarely made any reference to her death and did not give any serious instructions for her funeral: "Bury me in the back garden—this body is only my shell. I myself will be more alive than I have ever been."

The days passed by and Tante Corrie kept up with her work admirably. I often wondered at the phenomenon of a young spirit encased in such an old body. With the coming of spring of that year an increasing amount of time was given to the making of films. Jim Collier, director of "The Hiding Place" movie became one of her greatest friends. He believed that her main gift was her imagination, that ability to conceive a vision and turn it into reality. And since he too possessed the gift in no small measure, the two of them identified quickly. They spent hours together in the sitting room of Shalom House, or on the patio if the sun was shining, discussing the scripts of forthcoming movies. I liked Jimmy; I could see that he was employing all the gifts of his sensitive artistic nature in an effort to interpret Tante Corrie's desires and put them on film. He, too, was working in an intense way, as if underlining the sense that there was much to do in a short time.

The second short film was to be made with Christian American Indians. Tante Corrie had had a relationship with them for some time, and was deeply committed to their cause. The previous year the Christian Indians had honored her at a ceremony in Flagstaff, Arizona, receiving her as a member of their tribes, giving her a Hopi name and an Indian headdress and shawl. These items were placed carefully by Tante Corrie on the wall of the guest room in Shalom House together with a wooden plaque, stating: "Corrie ten Boom—prisoner of the Lord Jesus Christ." The plaque had been made for her by the inmates at San Quentin. These were the kinds of honors that pleased her most. She had received several high distinctions, none perhaps greater, humanly speaking, than the one from the Queen of the Netherlands proclaiming her a Knight of the Order of Orange-Nassau. However, this certificate and accompanying medal were kept in a drawer, never on display and rarely talked about.

After the honors she received at Flagstaff, Tante Corrie began to pray more regularly for the Indian tribes, asking God to use her to help them in their difficult circumstances. Now the opportunity had arisen to reenact that ceremony on film. Again, as with the prisoners, I noticed that when she began to pray in a specific way for others, God put her in a position to help them.

Tante Corrie and I had fun while she learned all she could about the medium of film. We bought some makeup, a simple powder compact, and a lipstick. Her olive, suntanned skin did not require much enhancing. Next we sorted through her wardrobe and decided that she needed a couple of dresses in colors and styles suitable for the cameras. At the local shopping mall we bought an informal dress in soft pastel colors, and one in a plain navy blue classic style.

After several weeks of work on the script by Jim Collier and Tante Corrie, we traveled to the filming location in Arizona. She spent hours beforehand trying to memorize her lines. I was aware that this was an extremely hard exercise for her, more difficult than the year before when she had made the film for prisoners. I knew she was concerned, for although she could use a teleprompter some of the time, there were to be many scenes when its use would not be possible. With the same expectancy that always attended her prayers, Tante Corrie lifted her hands and said, "Father, thank You that I can go forth in Your strength. Give a special anointing of Your Holy Spirit so that I will be able to do the necessary work. Help me to remember the lines, Lord. Use this movie to help the American Indians and to cause many Christians to become aware of their needs. Thank You. Hallelujah! Amen."

We were met at Phoenix Airport by Tom Claus, leader of CHIEF (Christian Hope Indian Eskimo Fellowship), who drove us to the hotel. Filming was to begin the next day. Because Tante Corrie no longer traveled constantly and had rested up before leaving Shalom House, she had decided not to take the two-day break before starting this new assignment.

The next afternoon saw us at the bottom of a mountainside far removed from noise and traffic and the press of people, so much part of life in Placentia. The dome of the sky seemed so much higher than in California and it was so very blue. The air was fresh and clean, the desert green and full of blooming cacti. In order to reach the chosen site for a filmed discussion between Tante Corrie and Tom Claus, a steep climb up this sandy steep hillside was necessary. I knew it would be too much for her.

"Tante Corrie, will you please take that climb very slowly?"

"Ja," she replied, taking the arms of two of the crew and beginning her ascent. I followed them slowly, carrying the script and an Indian blanket. There was a stiff breeze and it was cool.

"I believe I have to stop," said Tante Corrie, rather out of breath after a few yards and a long way from the filming site.

The crew quickly solved the problem. Seating her in a wooden chair, four of them each took a chair leg, hoisted it several feet from the ground and carried her up.

Crew and cameras in position, Tom Claus and Tante Corrie began their discussion. There were many retakes. Patiently they started again. The wind blew more strongly, disturbing her hair. Those responsible for continuity of the film kept an eye on such detail between shots and I restored her hairstyle as needed. At several points she could not use a teleprompter because of the angle of filming, so we wrote out her lines on large pieces of cardboard and held them up for her to read. The wind became stronger and colder. In between scenes we wrapped Tante Corrie in the Indian blanket. A little cactus wren viewed us with suspicion from her low nest a few feet away, but she bravely stayed to guard her eggs.

Filming completed, Tante Corrie was carried down the mountain again and driven to her hotel room where she worked on tomorrow's lines. It was going to be a much more exacting day.

The next day was Tante Corrie's eighty-sixth birthday. The hotel operator woke us at 6:30 a.m. and we left early to join the Indians for a full day of filming. This was to be the reenactment of the ceremony in which she received an Indian name. The site was near a creek with mountains in the background, lush green, quiet, and the air was pure and fragrant. The Indians were very helpful and friendly. They had built a campfire and prepared a bed for Tante Corrie in the shade so that she could rest between scenes. The reenactment of the ceremony was very moving, taking place around the campfire, with Indians dressed in their colorful regalia. I could see that Tante Corrie was enjoying herself immensely, tired as she was. I noticed that she retreated to her bed in the shade at every opportunity to regain strength for the next scenes. It was all the more amazing then that she had the strength that evening to invite several people to her room to spend a little while celebrating her birthday.

After four days of filming, we were driven to Phoenix Airport. She was installed in the squeakiest wheelchair I had yet encountered, and we laughed all the way to Gate 12, mainly, I know in my case, from relief that yet another mission had been completed.

If I had expected some days of relaxation at Shalom House, I was wrong. Immediately on arrival, the busy routine continued relentlessly. The telephone rang, visitors arrived, letters piled up, and tension rose in me. Tante Corrie was very tired and had to take several extra days in bed. I wrestled inwardly, wanting to be a servant, yet thinking, *how unfair it is of all these people to make demands on her, and at the same time, make demands on me.*

Three months had passed since my last discussion with Tante Corrie about the fact that I often felt overwhelmed and out of place in my role as servant, and here I was, still struggling with the issue. I knew that the time had come when the matter had to be resolved once and for all. Why in the world was I feeling so off-balance? I asked myself. I loved Tante Corrie, believed in her message, knew she was a gift to the world in this century, and had deliberately chosen to stay with her. Why was I bridling at my role? I felt that I could not go to Tante Corrie again with the problem. She was very tired, and because her visionary mind was so convinced of the vital importance of her message she could sometimes seem a little impatient; the answer was so clear to her. Her message was all-consuming and it had to be or she would never have been able to accomplish so much.

Judging by the lack of peace in my heart, I seriously considered if it was right to continue to stay with her and believed that the time had come to make a definite choice between staying or leaving.

Knowing that I needed time alone, I asked Tante Corrie for a day off, and, leaving her in the good hands of Elizabeth, headed toward the Pacific Ocean. There, I found a quiet place on a cliff and set up the deck chair I had brought along. It was a warm spring day, the sky and the sea were deep blue and the semi-tropical flowers and shrubs splashed color everywhere.

"Father," I prayed, "I need to come to grips with my problem and find perspective and proportion in this extraordinary role You have given me. I know that You cannot make mistakes, but it seems to me that I am not really in the right place. I am asking You to speak to me about it. And if by the end of this day I have no clear word from You, I am going to assume that I was wrong in thinking You had given me a life commitment and that You have another much better person in mind to help Tante Corrie."

After a time of watching the ocean and smelling the salt breeze, I heard God speak to me inside and what he said was something like this:

I want you to remember some instances from this last year with Tante Corrie in Shalom House. Put them into the framework of a typical day with her and look at that day as it were from a heavenly perspective.

I settled back in my deck chair, closed my eyes and let my mind go back over the past year. Recollection after recollection crowded in, and I found myself reliving, as it were, a day in our lives, not a literal day because the instances had not taken place in any set twenty-four hours, but it could well be described as typical in its intensity.

I saw myself entering Tante Corrie's room with her morning tea and on this day she was quiet and serious: "I had a dream last night," she said. "I dreamed I was speaking to prisoners and did not have a message. They walked away. Then I prayed, 'Lord, that is how I am without You. But with You I do have a message and can complete the books and films.' "

We also prayed together before the day's activities began. "Lord, keep me close to Your heart," she said in her daily prayer, "so that I see things as it were more and more from Your point of view."

In my mind's eye I followed Tante Corrie down the corridor from her bedroom to the living room. The stoop in her shoulders was much more noticeable now. She took her usual walk in the garden before starting work, checking that the bird feeders were full and that the hummingbirds had enough nectar. I remembered her joy on that day when she had discovered the first tiny fruit on the little orange tree.

She settled down to work at her desk, poring over one of her current manuscripts. I knew she would not be able to keep at it for long, because we were soon to be invaded by a group of thirty-two teenagers from a local church. When they arrived, I scurried around to find soft drinks and cookies as they settled down in the living room. Tante Corrie sat in the green reclining chair, the boys and girls filled the white sofa and the floor, looking at her eagerly. What a lot of questions they had asked.

"What is the key to brokenness?"

"Lose your life for Jesus' sake. It seems that you lose it, but you gain it."

"What did David mean in Psalm 51 when he said, 'Do not take thy Holy Spirit from me'? Is this possible?"

"We live this side of Pentecost. We know in the New Testament more about the Holy Spirit than David knew. Study all that is written in the New Testament. It does not take away from Psalm 51 but fulfills it. There are some truths in the Bible that seem to be contradictions, but they are not; we only cannot understand them with our logical thinking. Compare Scripture with Scripture and ask the Holy Spirit to help you."

"Am I really, truly, my brother's keeper?"

"You surely are, and you know it. Talk it over with the Lord."

In her typical manner of not allowing visitors to stay longer than her strength permitted, after an hour-and-a-half she brought the visit to a definite close by saying, "Now we pray," praying immediately, and then taking leave of her visitors.

I accompanied the teenagers to the front door, made a few telephone calls, and then Tante Corrie, Elizabeth, and I sat down to lunch, after which I said to Tante Corrie, "How about taking a really good rest now? Let me take the phone off the hook for thirty minutes."

"No, child, we must be available. It could be that somebody in need will call us."

After thirty minutes of rest she emerged, carrying a little bottle of nitroglycerine. I knew that her heart had been troubling her.

"I have a horrible feeling just here," she said, pressing her hand to the left side of her chest. "This must be what it feels like to die."

Returning to her manuscript, Tante Corrie was interrupted at some point by a telephone call. For instance, an evangelist, well-known in his own eastern country, telephoned and asked if he could visit her. She was delighted to hear from him, as she had worked with him with much blessing in the past.

"What a joy to see you," she beamed upon his arrival. "But what brings you to the United States?"

The man told her that his church had raised the money to send him for medical investigation in California, because his health was giving cause for concern. Examination in Los Angeles the week before had revealed a brain tumor.

"Tante Corrie, will you pray that the Lord will heal me?"

She did, in a very matter-of-fact and simple way. (At this point I stepped out of my framework of a twenty-four hour period and remembered that a few days later the evangelist appeared on the doorstep excitedly waving some X-rays that had just been taken. There was no sign of the tumor. Tante Corrie thanked God and was very humbled by the incident. She asked him and anyone else who knew about it not to publicize the matter. She did not want anybody to get the idea that she had a special gift of healing.)

Over supper, after the visitor had left, I said, "Tante Corrie, won't you consider not going to the prison prayer meeting this evening? You really are too tired."

"I am feeling quite a bit better now. It is all right. Let's go to the meeting, but be sure to leave before it gets late."

I opened my eyes and was back on the cliff overlooking the ocean. It was as if I suddenly woke up and began to see Tante Corrie's life from the viewpoint of the heavenlies. Here was a warrior who was having to slow down, but who really did not know it yet. Her energies were leaving her. God knew it, but she was not fully aware of it. I caught a glimpse as never before of the tenderness of the Lord in preparing her for a diminishing of her energies by giving her a home from which to work, and I saw too that all this was for my sake as well. He wanted me to be the person who saw what it was like when energies are diminishing, who saw how He dealt with His children at those times. I saw that somehow this was a training ground and I felt very sure that there could be no question of my leaving her. The matter had been resolved and was finally settled.

When I arrived back at Shalom House Tante Corrie showed her usual interest in my day.

"You stepped into the car," she said, "what happened next?"

I described to her the beautiful ocean scene but did not confide in her about my talk with the Lord.

Later that week she and I went for a walk in the neighborhood. We set off toward a small park. Tante Corrie held onto my left elbow with her right hand and we walked in step with each other. As we went, she talked about her two previous companions whom she had loved very much— Connie, who had accompanied her all over the world, and Ellen, who had been with her for the nine years previous to my joining Tante Corrie. She told me how the Lord had led both Connie and Ellen into marriage.

"But we," said Tante Corrie, as we stepped off the pavement near Grady and Maurine's house, "we will be together until the end. Or rather, until the wonderful new beginning."

And I knew that she was right. But how did she know?

Spring turned to summer and our energies and attentions were focused on another film, "Jesus Is Victor: A

Personal Portrait of Corrie ten Boom." Filming took place in various locations according to the script's needs. One scene required a rose garden. A large and beautiful burial place called Rose Hills Memorial Park provided just the right setting. In June of 1978 the roses were in full bloom, ideal for filming.

How does she manage it? I wondered for the hundredth time, as I watched Tante Corrie trying to learn her lines and prepare for the filming. The day chosen for filming was extremely hot, and, what was worse, smoggy. After several hours, it hurt to breathe and our eyes were stinging. We discovered a seat in a shady rose bower and turned it into a little hiding place to which Tante Corrie retreated between scenes. Director, crew, helpers, and star became warmer and warmer. There were many retakes.

"Action!" said Jimmy Collier, and time and again what would otherwise have been a perfect "take" had to be scrapped because the sound man indicated the intrusion of noise above Tante Corrie's voice. That day the sound technicians had to deal with noise from trains, planes, long funeral processions, trucks, lawn mowers and gardeners. And then there were the interruptions from people. At one point conditions seemed perfect. There was no external noise. Tante Corrie was feeling refreshed, having just had a short rest, and was now standing in front of the cameras ready to walk down an avenue of roses, teleprompter in position, all the crew members and all extra staff members out of sight.

"Action!" said the director, and silently I prayed that this would capture the essence of what was to be conveyed by this scene. The temperature had hit ninety-five degrees and the air was heavy with smog. Tante Corrie in her pink dress, among pink and red roses, began to speak. Suddenly a bus bearing the words *Salvation Army* and the name of a nearby oceanside town swept through the gates, came to a noisy halt, and discharged a large number of excited, elderly ladies obviously on a day's outing. Their excitement mounted as they spied a familiar figure a few yards away surrounded by filming equipment.

"Corrie ten Boom," called out one determined lady. She strode forward, holding out her hand. "How wonderful to meet you." About to enter into animated conversation, she was interrupted by a fit of coughing. "Oh, this terrible smog," she complained, "I don't know how anyone can live here."

"They don't live here," said Tante Corrie, pointing toward the graveyard, "everybody is dead here."

The ladies from the bus having been escorted off our natural film set, filming commenced yet again. One thing after another brought interruptions. The day was rather like an obstacle race. I watched the proceedings with some anxiety, recalling a morning recently when Tante Corrie had again told me that her heart was troubling her.

However, she not only had the energy to give attention to the lady from the bus, when the day's work was complete she wanted to celebrate by eating supper at a Pancake House on the way home.

The familiar sigh of relief welled up inside me as I pulled the car into the garage that night.

She made it through another grueling session, I thought thankfully. *But I have got to protect her. How can I do it most effectively?*

The next day seemed to be full of confusion, with all kinds of unnecessary interruptions. I had noticed that when she was particularly involved in a book or film project there tended to be times like this. Tante Corrie immediately recognized it for what it was, a spiritual attack. She was constantly aware of the spiritual battle.

"Let's pray," she said as I stood by her desk. "The devil

knows that his time is short. We are not fighting against flesh and blood but against principalities and powers. There is the devil, much stronger than I, but there is Jesus, much stronger than the devil, and together with Him, I will win." In the name of the Lord Jesus she prayed against the devil's attacks.

I hoped that the day would soon come when the spiritual gift of discernment was mine in greater measure. It was a much better thing to pray against the cause of spiritual attack than to try to protect her from its physical manifestations.

In the summer of 1978, when Tante Corrie had been in her house for eighteen months, her friend and publisher Bill Barbour came to visit her once again. They sat together on the patio after Bill had been given a tour of the garden by Tante Corrie. It was a real garden now, I noted with considerable satisfaction. Tante Corrie's favorite orange tree was both growing taller and spreading its little branches, the bougainvillaea was forming a green covering to the fence, the rose bushes were blooming.

Bill told Tante Corrie that a special version of "This is Your Life," with herself as the subject, was being planned for mid-July in Denver. Her publisher and World Wide Pictures were planning this honor for her. I wondered how she would respond. It was indeed a nice idea, but I knew that Denver had a high altitude. How would her heart stand up to that? Tante Corrie, however, accepted enthusiastically.

We took a trip into the California mountains, traveling to a height equal to that of Denver to see how she withstood the test physically. There were no problems, so we boarded the flight to Denver in mid-July with considerable anticipation.

While Tante Corrie rested in her hotel room, guests flew in from various parts of the country and from Europe. Their names were kept secret from her until almost the last moment. Cliff Barrows was master of ceremonies. Tante

Corrie wore a long evening gown in soft green for the occasion. Seated on the sofa of the stage set, she was greeted by many of the people, past and present, in whose lives she had played an important role, and they, in many cases, in hers. There was her nephew, Peter van Woerden from Switzerland; Hans Poley, a partner in the underground work in Holland during the war; Truus Benes, one of the staff of the Deaconess House that received Tante Corrie directly after her release from Ravensbruck; Joni Eareckson; Lotte Reimeringer, who had been her secretary in Holland just after the war; Tom Claus wearing his Indian headdress; Ruth Graham; and many others.

During the course of the evening, Cliff Barrows referred to a comment she had once made during a visit to his home: "When people come up and give me a compliment—'Corrie, that was a good talk,' or 'Corrie, you were so brave,' I take each remark as if it were a flower. At the end of each day I lift up the bouquet of flowers I have gathered throughout the day and say, 'Here you are, Lord, it is all Yours.' "

At the end of this tribute in Denver, after an evening full of emotional memories, looking back over a very full eighty-six years, Tante Corrie was presented with a large bouquet of yellow roses. As the crowd stood to applaud her, she lifted the bouquet to the Lord and I knew she was saying to Him, "Lord Jesus, this is Yours."

She returned to Placentia feeling fairly well, although the altitude of Denver had in fact proved too much for her old heart. On the second day it had been necessary to enlist the help of a tank of oxygen.

Her friend of many years, Lotte Reimeringer, came back to Placentia with us. Tante Corrie was clearly very fond of Lotte, who was in her late sixties and deceptively delicate-looking. "Have you noticed what lovely eyes Lotte has?" said Tante Corrie to me one evening. The purpose of Lotte's coming with us was for a vacation for her, but the next weeks saw the arrival of many guests. At one point all the beds in the house were filled and someone was even sleeping in the office. Lotte helped with the cooking and with any work that needed to be done. She was particularly gifted at helping Tante Corrie with her manuscripts, having had considerable practice at it in recent years at Tante Corrie's request and having the distinct advantage of being fluent in Dutch, English, and German. Tante Corrie discussed with Lotte the latest project that had been brought to her attention—the writing of a second daily devotional book as a sequel to *Each New Day*. The new book was to have the title, *This Day Is the Lord's*. Tante Corrie asked Lotte if she would consider coming back to the States from Holland for a certain time to help her with the book, and Lotte, although committed to her work as secretary at the headquarters of the Moravian Church in Holland at the time, was very willing to come. She worked hard during her "vacation," helping with the assembling of notes for the manuscript.

The pastors and members of nearby Rose Drive Friends Church gave Tante Corrie and me a great deal of practical love and support during the years at Placentia. Although she did not regularly attend any particular local church, she went to Rose Drive Church with Lotte and me on the first Sunday of August that summer. The senior pastor, seeing her in his congregation asked if she would like to give the people a few words of encouragement. Tante Corrie complied gladly. Slowly she made her way to the front, where she brought a short message and asked the church to pray for her. I prayed hard as she stood at the podium. Again and again she had to search for words.

In mid-August we put Lotte on the plane back to The Netherlands. There were no other guests in the house and for the first time in many weeks, Tante Corrie and I were alone again. In the coming days I worked hard typing out the ninety-nine completed pages of her new manuscript. A week after Lotte's departure we attended our weekly prayer meeting for prisoners in Grady and Maurine's home. That evening we had a particularly blessed time in prayer.

Tante Corrie also told us about a dearly loved minister who had served in Haarlem when she was a child. She remembered she must have been very small at the time he was there, because she climbed onto his lap when he came to visit the family, and on the day he told her that he was leaving the city to go to a new church she had cried. He comforted her and said, "Corrie, look up. People look up. Animals look down." She reminded those of us at the prayer meeting that we must always look up toward the Lord Jesus.

So summer, 1978, brought a large, public meeting in Denver, Colorado, a regular church service at Yorba Linda, California, a small prayer meeting in our neighbors' home— and Corrie ten Boom's long and varied public ministry came to a close.

7.

"Unless a Grain of Wheat Falls ..."

For several days Tante Corrie had complained about a bad headache, indicating especially her left temple. She spent a couple of days in bed. Returning her lunchtray to the kitchen one afternoon, I decided to have a few words with Elizabeth about it.

"I think that these headaches are caused by the busy schedule, don't you?" I asked as she cleared up the kitchen.

"Well, they certainly could be," she replied. "I've never known anyone at eighty-six who could take that tiring trip last month and then spend these past weeks engrossed in a manuscript. Let's hope that she is able to sleep this afternoon."

Our hope was fulfilled. Uncharacteristically, Tante Corrie slept for most of the rest of the day, livening up in the evening. We talked and prayed together, and she said to the Lord: "Father, will You protect our house and us this night and keep us so close to Your heart that even our dreams are peaceful."

Her head was still hurting, and she prepared to go to sleep early. I told her that I was going to bed early myself. We said goodnight. When my few chores were finished, I went to my room, noting that Tante Corrie's light had been turned out. I heard nothing for the rest of the night.

When I got up the next morning I could see as I looked along the corridor from my room to hers that all was still in darkness. She had not drawn back the heavy drapes across the large window facing east, so I knew she had not been watching the sunrise as she usually did. All was quiet.

I went to the sitting room with my Bible. My reading that day was John 13, which tells about how the Lord of glory "knowing that the Father had put all things under his power, and that he had come from God and was returning to God" stood up from His meal, took a towel and began to wash and dry the disciples' feet. Peter, who did not understand, protested. I sympathized with him; servanthood was a hard role to understand. I still had much to learn. I recalled how often it had been necessary during the last two years with Tante Corrie to lay aside my own desires and be willing to work through the desires of somebody else—my very strong leader. But lately there had been more peace in my heart than ever before. I was learning that when I prayed for the power of the Holy Spirit to fulfill my role of servant, He gave that power, or love, patience, joy, peace—whatever I needed at a given moment.

I recalled praying a short while before, "Lord, will You do whatever is necessary in my life to make me a more godly woman?"

I wonder if I would have prayed that prayer if I had known what God's answer would be. He was about to lead me into the greatest lesson on servanthood that I had ever known.

The house was peaceful, Tante Corrie's room still dark. I was happy that she was getting some extra sleep and I read on.

"When he had finished washing their feet, he put on his clothes and returned to his place. 'Do you understand what I have done for you?' he asked them. 'You call me "Teacher" and "Lord," and rightly so, for that is what I am. Now that I, your Lord and Teacher, have washed your feet, you also should wash one another's feet. I have set you an example that you should do as I have done for you.'"

Noticing that the hands of the little brown mantle clock were pointing to nearly 8 a.m., I decided it was time to make a cup of tea and wake Tante Corrie.

Her room was still dark, so I went in quietly, placed the tray carefully on the table and went to pull the drapes, my back toward the bed.

The sunlight flooded in, and I said, "Good morning, Tante Corrie," thinking it unusual in the couple of seconds it took to straighten the curtains that she was not yet awake enough to respond to my greeting.

I turned to face her bed, and for a moment I froze.

In front of me, lying on her back, her chin pressed into her chest at a strange angle, lay Tante Corrie. She looked up at me with agonized blue eyes and an expression that could only be described as pleading.

I ran to her bedside, fell on my knees beside her and took hold of her right hand. It was cold and limp and did not respond to my grasp.

"What is the matter, Tante Corrie?"

No response. For a fleeting moment the thought came, *Are you playing a game with me?* Tante Corrie was never at a loss for words.

"Can you tell me, Tante Corrie?" I felt the warm breeze from the window and the morning sun on my back. The only sound coming from Tante Corrie was a labored, rattling sound in her throat as she breathed. Her eyes continued to look straight into mine.

"Let's pray, Tante Corrie."

Immediately she closed her eyes, but where was the familiar uplifting of her hands?

"Father, in the name of Jesus I ask You to put Your hand on Tante Corrie and to heal her of whatever is wrong with her. Thank You. Amen."

Tante Corrie opened her eyes. I regarded her in shocked

silence for a moment. Whatever was wrong? Was this a heart attack? I really had no idea.

It was just after 8 a.m. Elizabeth would not be arriving for a whole hour. There had to be some action before then. Running to the telephone I summoned a friend who lived close by. She arrived very quickly and seeing my shocked appearance took things in hand.

"I'll call an ambulance while you go and get dressed." I had forgotten that I was still in my robe.

Flinging on some clothes and running a comb through my hair I was amazed at the quick arrival of the ambulance. I heard the loud thuds as a stretcher was taken out of the vehicle, the squeak of Shalom House's iron gate as the ambulance men came up the walkway. I rushed to the door to let them in and they moved into Tante Corrie's room, lifting her onto a stretcher. Her eyes were closed. She did not seem to know what was taking place and made no protest.

The tray with two cups of cold tea was still on the table and I saw something I had not noticed earlier. Several books had been knocked off her bedside table and were lying on the floor. It must have happened during the night, and I had heard nothing. Why had she not called me? Had she not been able to? How long had she been lying there waiting for me to arrive? Why hadn't I realized that something was terribly wrong?

The ambulance men were carrying her out of her room now, down the corridor, and outside where the stretcher was loaded into the waiting vehicle. "May I sit next to her?" I asked the ambulance driver. On being told that I would have to sit in front, I said, "Tante Corrie, I am going with you to the hospital, but I will have to ride in front."

No response.

The short drive seemed to take hours. Every light was red. *Why doesn't the driver turn on the emergency lights and his siren?*

I thought, *Tante Corrie could be dying.* For some reason I did not ask him. It felt to me as though I were dreaming and watching a scene that was not really taking place in actual life.

After a few minutes we arrived at the hospital where Tante Corrie had had the pacemaker operation the previous year, and she was taken straight to the emergency room. I was not allowed to go with her, and took the opportunity to use the telephone and inform a few of her friends of what had happened—Elizabeth, Grady, and Maurine, our prayer partner neighbors, and a few members of the board.

Tante Corrie was immediately referred to the care of an internist, and I waited in the lobby and remembered the last occasion I had been here—waiting for the results of the pacemaker operation last year. It was a spacious place with comfortable chairs, the receptionist's desk to the left, and a glass cupboard containing flowers for purchase on the right.

Before long the friends I had telephoned began to arrive. And after what seemed an endless time of waiting, the internist came out.

"Corrie has had a stroke," he said.

So that was it. I had often heard of the condition, but had never seen it close up.

"However did it happen?" I asked him.

He explained to me that a stroke occurs when there is an interruption in the blood supply to the brain. There could be many reasons for this, but in an old person like Tante Corrie the reason is most likely to be that the blood vessels to the brain gradually become clogged and finally fill up completely for a while, causing the flow of blood to the brain to stop for a period of time, resulting in brain damage.

"What are her symptoms?" I asked.

"She has partial right-sided paralysis and has lost her ability to speak. She has been transferred to the intensive care

99

unit and we will know more by this evening. But because of her age, I think her chances of pulling through this are not very good."

Why had I not seen this coming? I asked myself. I might have been able to do something to prevent it.

Tante Corrie's friends and I assembled outside intensive care and I was told that as soon as she was settled I could go in to be with her for a while. How glad I was to see the familiar faces of Elizabeth, board members who had become friends, and Grady and Maurine, so much a part of life at Shalom House. Finally a nurse came to admit me to ICU. Inside the double doors I passed a nurses' center where the staff monitored their patients' vital signs on a bank of screens glowing with electronic symbols. The nurse led me into a cubicle, and there lay Tante Corrie with her eyes closed. Her face was very pallid, and she was wearing a white cotton hospital gown tied with strings behind her neck. A needle had been inserted into a vein in her right hand and fastened there with tape. It was attached to a piece of tubing leading to a bottle in which, now and then, a bubble floated to the top of a clear liquid.

"Why does she have an IV?" I asked the nurse.

"It is to prevent her from becoming dehydrated," she explained. "She can't swallow properly at the moment."

The nurse left and I sat down next to Tante Corrie. It seemed very unreal to be talking to a nurse about her in her presence and not have her respond. She always had things under control. It was unthinkable that she could not even request a drink of water. She was so strangely still. Did she know I was with her? Taking her left hand, the one unaffected by the stroke, I began to talk to her: "Tante Corrie, can you hear me?"

She did not reply or respond in any way. Her face was grayish-white. I could not get over the shock of seeing this vital and communicative leader in a state of such complete inertia. I sat silently praying for her. And after a few minutes, I joined the friends outside and reported to them.

All day the vigil continued. I went into Tante Corrie's cubicle as often as I was permitted. Once or twice she opened her eyes. They were putty-colored and expressionless. She still did not seem to know that I was there. I was sure she was going to die.

During the day her friends and I tried to deal with the troubling question that many must face at times like this. How were we to pray? There was a comfortable sitting area just outside ICU and we talked together in hushed voices because it seemed to be the correct thing to do in these somber circumstances. How *shall* we pray? we wondered. It did not seem right to pray for her release in death, but it also did not seem right to pray that she stay on earth if she was going to remain in the condition she was in.

Five o'clock arrived and the internist came, as he had done on several occasions during the day, to check on her condition. He talked to several of us as we stood in the waiting area and said: "I think that, because she has got through this day, she has a fifty-fifty chance of recovering."

"Is there anything I could have done to stop this happening?" I asked him.

"No," was his reply, "once a stroke is in progress, nothing can be done to prevent it."

The next day Tante Corrie began to regain consciousness, and during part of my time with her in ICU I thought she recognized me although she still could not talk or move her right leg or right arm. She seemed very restless and anxious at times and plucked at the sheet with her left hand. It was quite frightening to see her behaving in a way that was so out of character with the normal Tante Corrie.

As often as I could, I talked to the nurses and gained

quite a lot of information about strokes. It was explained to me that the damage caused to the brain results in the swelling of that organ. Since the encasing skull means that there is no way for the pressure thus created to be relieved until the damage begins to heal, there is irritation to the brain lining. This results in symptoms beyond the control of the patient— for example, frequent movement of the unparalyzed limbs, and an anxious, almost angry attitude.

The nurses also told me that although stroke patients can hear the sounds of the words being said to them, they often cannot make sense of the words. It will come across to them as a foreign language and perhaps they can catch one or two of the words, doing their best to make sense of it. It was important to speak slowly and as clearly as possible. I was also told that stroke patients often cannot reply appropriately to a question. When they mean "no" they often say "yes" and vice-versa. Although some stroke patients were unable to speak, one nurse explained, surprisingly they were sometimes able to sing if they heard a tune they knew well. Somehow tunes were stored in an undamaged part of the brain and somehow the memory of the tune evoked the memory of the words although nobody knew quite how. I was beginning to discover that not a great deal of information has been gathered about the functions of the brain.

On the evening of August 25, after two extremely long days, a Dutch-speaking friend and I were with her in ICU and decided to sing together an old Dutch hymn, one of Tante Corrie's favorites, based on Psalm 42: "As pants the hart for cooling streams, so longs my soul for You, O God." I was combing her hair as we sang, when suddenly, almost unbelievably, we saw her lips move and heard her joining in with the melody and a few words of the hymn. We were overjoyed, and Tante Corrie seemed to be able to catch something of our mood.

"We love you, Tante Corrie," we told her, "and we know you love us." An expression of assent—as clear as if she had said "yes"—appeared on her face.

After two days, a definite contact had been made.

The hours passed slowly and Tante Corrie became more conscious although she slept a good deal of the time. Her friends and I took turns keeping her company as often as we were allowed in ICU. We talked to her, read portions of the Bible, and prayed with her aloud. If Tante Corrie heard us, there was no response.

After three days in ICU the decision was taken to move her to a side ward and I watched while Tante Corrie was wheeled out into the corridor, accompanied by her IV, and taken to a small, oblong room containing two beds, a sink, and a television mounted on a shelf near the ceiling. Although it was a large enough room for two patients I was glad that the other bed was not occupied. It was a relief to be out of the atmosphere of ICU with its constant bleeping noises and into a place where we could be alone.

I was also happy to see that a little movement was returning to Tante Corrie's right leg and foot. The right arm was still immobile and flaccid. I continued to read to her from the Bible and talk to her. There were times when she understood what was said to her, but usually she apparently could not: "It is Sunday, Tante Corrie, and it is midday."

No response.

"You had a stroke last Wednesday, that is why you are here in the hospital. The doctor says you are improving."

Her eyes opened and looked into mine, but without any expression of understanding.

One evening, six days after the stroke, having talked to Lotte in Holland for the second time since this illness began, I parked the car in the warm August evening and entered the much cooler air conditioning of the hospital building. Passing through the now-familiar lobby, I made my way to Tante Corrie's room.

She was alone and lying on her back, wearing the white cotton hospital gown. When I reached her side, she stretched out her left hand to grasp my right one tightly, looked up at me with eyes full of distress and desperation, and with tremendous effort managed to form two words: "Hilf mir." "Help me," spoken in the German language.

There was something in the way she said it and the fact that it was in German, not Dutch, that made me shudder. It seemed to me that, in her confusion, she thought she was back in concentration camp, back in a horrifying imprisonment and was appealing to one of her guards for help.

"Oh, Tante Corrie," I said, nearly choking on the words, "I do wish I could help you more." My vigorous leader was a prisoner within her own body.

At home that night, I racked my brain, trying to remember what Tante Corrie had told me about her own communication with her mother who died in 1921 after having been a stroke victim for many years. I reread those parts of her books that referred to her attempts to communicate. She had told me that she would ask a question while holding her finger on her mother's pulse. If there was a variation in the speed of the pulse it was often an indication that her mother had understood. Tante Corrie's pacemaker did not allow her heart rate to drop below seventy-two beats per minute, but her heart would often beat on its own at a consistently higher rate. I thought I would try that method, too.

The next morning I went into her room with raised hopes. The room was much less bare now. Several beautiful bouquets of flowers had been delivered.

Tante Corrie was awake, and I thought she understood my *Good morning*. I sat down beside her and took her left hand, putting my finger over her pulse. Slowly I began to ask questions: "Tante Corrie, can you hear me?"

No expression of assent, no change in pulse rate.

"Do you understand that you have had a stroke?"

Still no change in pulse rate.

I posed a few more questions, but soon had to admit defeat. What had worked for her mother was not working for her.

A week had passed since the stroke. Tante Corrie ate very little, and still had her IV. She was allowed visitors in moderation, and to my amazement the nurses began to transfer her from her bed to a wheelchair. It looked much too strenuous, but they assured me that it was better for her to get up for a while each day. I accepted that, but found it much harder to understand why, when I entered her room, I often found the television blaring. Tante Corrie would be lying with her eyes closed. She rarely watched television when she was well. How tiring the noise must be to her. I asked the nurses why it had been turned on, and they explained that it was necessary to stimulate Tante Corrie's brain and to employ every device possible to help her relate to her surroundings in order to be restored to a normal life.

When the specialist made his next check on Tante Corrie I asked if I could talk to him, and we stepped into the corridor outside her room.

"Doctor, I need to know more about what to expect for the future."

"I'm afraid I can't tell you that," he replied, "each stroke patient is different."

"But what are the general prospects?"

"Well, there is a definite improvement in the paralysis. I think she is going to be able to walk again and to regain the use of her right hand and arm. An important thing to look for now is how quickly she regains her speech," he said with emphasis. "If she begins to talk again soon that is a good sign. The longer the time that passes without the return of speech, the less likely it is that it *will* return."

"Can she come home again?"

"Yes, when she is able to eat and drink adequately and has regained more mobility."

"What is her life expectancy?"

"That's impossible for me to say. As you know, she is eighty-six years old now. She could live for a few days or a few years."

That afternoon while Tante Corrie slept, I thought about the doctor's words. Along with the general prognosis, he had said she might live for a few days or a few years—and I had a life commitment to her. I remembered how, after the pressures mounted, I had felt I had the freedom to leave, but made the decision to stay. I had joined Tante Corrie when she was strong and healthy, but things were very different now. I saw why God had given me the freedom to leave. When I made the decision to stay "for better or for worse" it was a free will choice. And suddenly, I was aware that God's sense of timing had touched my life as it had always touched Corrie's. For now, a clearheaded decision would have been impossible.

The hours at the hospital passed slowly. Time was on our side at first. I was glad that Tante Corrie had lived and was improving to some degree. But time was becoming an enemy. Speech was not returning and the doctor had said that the longer it took for speech to return, the less likely it was that it would return adequately at all.

After several days, a group of friends and board members, many of them ministers, went to her hospital room. She was conscious and they told her that they were going to pray for her and anoint her with oil according to the Bible's directions. My mind went back to the scene in Shalom House the year before when Tante Corrie had prayed for the minister with the brain tumor and God had healed him. What would happen now? Tante Corrie was prayed for, anointed with oil, and healing was claimed in the name of the Lord Jesus. Nothing appeared to happen.

But in the succeeding days she became stronger physically, began to eat more after having often refused food, and became fully conscious. She now understood many of the things said to her and responded sometimes with a nod of the head or with *ja* or *nee*. It was much easier for her to understand Dutch than English, and I translated a lot of messages into her ear, bending as near to her as possible.

As soon as Tante Corrie became consistently conscious, a speech pathologist came to carry out tests. She placed four objects on a tray in front of her—a key, a box of matches, a quarter, and a pen.

"Show me the key, Corrie," said the speech pathologist.

Tante Corrie looked confused. *Surely she knows which is the key,* I thought. *It must be that she cannot understand English.*

"Let me try it in Dutch," I offered.

"Tante Corrie, *wilt u de sleutel aanwijzen?"*

No response. She could not identify the key, the box of matches, or the quarter. When given the choice between the key and the pen she managed to identify the pen hesitatingly with her left hand. She did not enjoy the short session at all and I was glad when it was time for the speech pathologist to leave.

If only I could help her recognize something familiar, I thought as I drove home. And that evening I had a good idea, for a copy of her book, *Don't Wrestle, Just Nestle,* had just arrived from the printers. I felt certain she would recognize it and that it would make her very happy. *I will take it to her this evening and make a little celebration of it, I decided, just as I've seen her do on receiving the first copy of other books.*

Feeling a new lightheartedness, I entered her room that night more quickly than usual, the book in my hand.

"Look, Tante Corrie," I said triumphantly, "a baby has been born. Here is your very latest book, just printed!"

I expected her to reach out for it, but she did not. She looked at it with a face full of puzzlement, as if she had never seen a book in her life. I put it in her hand and she looked at the spine of the book and then turned to the front and back covers, regarding them slowly. With shock, I realized that it no longer made sense to her that the printed words inside the book had once been written by her. I took the book from her to avoid causing any concern about my enthusiasm and her lack of ability to respond. Why couldn't she understand?

Leaving her room, I went to talk privately with the speech pathologist.

She explained to me that Tante Corrie had a language disturbance called "aphasia," which happens frequently after a stroke. Aphasia occurs when there is injury to the dominant side of the brain. For most people this is the left hemisphere, and that was where Tante Corrie's brain injury had occurred. The problem called aphasia involves language in all its aspects—speech and the understanding of speech are affected, and so is the understanding of symbols, reading, writing, arithmetic, gestures. The therapist told me that the amount of impairment varied from patient to patient and that no two people had exactly the same brain injury symptoms. However, she emphasized, a *slow* regaining of communicative ability would not be a good sign. It was clear, then, that Tante Corrie no longer had the ability to speak and understand, nor could she read, write, interpret gestures, or make meaningful signs to those around her.

The therapist went on to explain that a common reaction to stroke patients is to think that they have become mentally deranged. Except in very extreme cases where judgment is impaired, however, the stroke patient remains him or her "self" and has the same intelligence. It is not a question of intellectual or emotional disturbance, but of language disturbance.

"When will we know more about the return of her speech?" I asked.

"Only time will tell," was her reply. "Each patient is different. You will have to work out your own communication system according to her rate of recovery or lack of recovery."

As I said good night to Tante Corrie that evening, I was suddenly aware of the strange shift taking place in our relationship. She had always been the leader, a long way out in front, the strong one, the one who spoke up. Now I had a new responsibility to try to interpret the desires that she had hitherto so clearly expressed—and not only that, but to take initiative on her behalf. I didn't dare think of the future. How long would this incapacity to communicate continue? And the Lord, though He felt very near at hand, was being silent, too.

As I walked through the hospital corridors on my way home that evening, I recalled a statement Tante Corrie repeated often, particularly when I was discouraged by setbacks, changes in the planned day, or yet more unexpected visitors: "Child, it is not as much what happens, but *how we take it* that is important. God is watching to see whether we allow the problems to defeat us, or whether we will go through them in His strength, being made stronger for the next problem and ultimately for the final end battle."

I walked outside into the warm September night, shivering at the change in temperature from the cool of the hospital building. It was very dark. And that was how the future looked. As I reached the car, I remembered another of Tante Corrie's statements: "Everything that happens to us in life is a training for the work we will do next."

If that was true, then this awful illness was not a big

setback or an interruption, but a stepping stone to even higher service.

I opened the car door, got in, and sat looking toward the hospital. Lying behind its walls was a very different Tante Corrie from the one I had known two weeks ago. But was she really different? She had retained the most essential part of her being—her relationship to the Lord Jesus Christ. That was surely the key to the fruit of her life. Because of her relationship to her Lord, she surrendered to His will time after time, not always without a struggle but yielding anyway, not always understanding but persevering in spite of that. It seemed to me, as I sat there in the quiet parking lot with a sudden awareness of the very real presence of God, that this could be the greatest trial in her life so far. And perhaps her greatest opportunity to glorify God.

In that dark night, I realized that God was not being silent after all.

8.

A Time to Weep

Tante Corrie continued to gain strength, and a physical therapist made daily visits to exercise her weakened right side. After two weeks, she was moving her right arm and right leg by herself and gradually was able to hold a cup and a fork. Such was the improvement in her paralysis that she began to wear her own nightgowns. Life was becoming more normal.

The great day arrived when the physical therapist helped her to stand and to take a few steps. Within several days she began to walk, leaning on her arm.

She, I, and her friends were overjoyed. Comparing her state of health to her condition on the day nearly three weeks before when she was carried into the hospital, we felt that remarkable progress had been made.

But I kept wondering, *What about her speech?* She could now understand a good deal more and life was clearly less confusing to her. She smiled and greeted visitors by turning toward them and holding out her hand and sometimes was even able to repeat *good morning* if it had first been said to her. However, there was absolutely no functional speech.

One evening, Tante Corrie looked at me very directly and pointed with her left index finger toward the door. I was beginning to learn that the use of that finger did not necessarily (although it might) indicate a particular direction. It was her way of letting me know that she had a question to which I needed to find an answer.

"Would you like something to drink?" She understood the question, but the answer was a shake of her head.

"Would you like something to eat?" She nodded and I went quickly to ask the nurse to prepare something.

When the tray came she pushed it away. It had not been what she wanted. I saw for the first time that day something the speech therapist had told me—that stroke patients often give inappropriate answers to questions.

The nurse took the food away and we started again. Finally, the question came: "Do you want to go home, Tante Corrie?" At once her eyes lit up and she nodded a very enthusiastic "yes."

"Let's ask the doctor about it at the next opportunity."

The next day the specialist examined her and was pleased with her progress: "I have heard you would like to go home, Corrie."

"Ja!" She found the word and even emphasized it by nodding her head.

"Then I think that if you continue doing this well you will be able to leave the hospital in two days' time. As soon as possible we will start you on speech lessons at home."

It was clear that Tante Corrie had understood all his words, but her concept of time was distorted. Each time I arrived in her room, she thought I had come to take her to Shalom House. At least, that is what I assumed by her eager pointings toward the door.

"Not yet, Tante Corrie," I told her. "You will be coming home tomorrow and we are getting everything ready for you."

Lots of questions arose in my mind. I was not a nurse. It looked as though she was going to be with us for a while yet. If she continued to live, how would I cope with this rather frighteningly different Tante Corrie? What about the half-finished projects back in Shalom House?

First things first, I reminded myself. Elizabeth and I needed to make some plans. We discussed some changes that would have to come. Because of weakened muscles on the right side of her throat, it would be hard for Tante Corrie to eat completely solid food at first. After consulting the dietitian at the hospital, we discussed the substance that would be suitable and planned meals accordingly. Tante Corrie could not be left alone at night, and we arranged a rotation of several friends who had volunteered to help.

Such was her progress that the next day she was actually able to step out of the car and walk by herself when we arrived at Shalom House.

We were greeted in the driveway by Elizabeth, several friends, and board members, all trying to keep their enthusiasm as low-key as possible so as not to overexcite her. The house was full of flowers: there were roses on the hall table, orchids from Hawaii on her desk, and various other floral arrangements from well-wishers all through the house. Tante Corrie went straight to her green reclining chair in the sitting room and sat down with a look of profound relief and contentment. She was home again at last.

She could not wait to spend time in her garden again. Later in the day when we were alone, we took a very short walk outside. She checked the birdfeeders and looked at the flowers. The vines were thick, the bougainvillaea was blooming now, and the roses were prolific. Even the little orange tree was making strides.

During her first days at home Tante Corrie was tired and slept a great deal. She did not like to be alone in this new and frightening world. I and several friends took turns being with her. I wondered how I would manage without all these supportive people.

I had not yet detected in my silent leader any attitude that balked at these strange new circumstances, although she sometimes seemed a little depressed. What I did notice was a sweetness and patience in her spirit that were there to a more marked degree than I had ever seen before. Time and again she tried to talk, but the result each time was a jumble of unassociated sounds, rarely an appropriate word. She could still say *yes* or *no* and *good morning* when the greeting had been made to her first. She could respond but not initiate speech.

I quickly discovered that Tante Corrie tired much more easily, she was much more likely than ever before to become emotionally overwrought, she needed far more sleep, her perception was distorted and she appeared to have become very fussy about the neat and orderly appearance of things. She straightened pictures and cushions the positions of which would never have bothered her before the stroke.

The physical body was a cumbersome imprisonment such as never before. Instead of diving into a day full of productive work she now needed a good deal of time just to get dressed. Tante Corrie, who used to be ready in the mornings before I was, now needed my help to get into her clothes.

Day by day, there was quite a bit of progress with her understanding. She was able to grasp much more of what was said than when she left the hospital a week before. One morning, having helped her dress in a blue dress and jacket and having fixed her silver hair, I followed her from her bedroom into the corridor. Her shoulders were even more stooped now, making her look very vulnerable. She had lost a lot of weight during her illness and the dress and jacket were much too big.

"We'll have to get you some new clothes, Tante Corrie."

"Ja," came the immediate response from ahead of me.

"Oh, Tante Corrie, you understood me the first time."

She stopped, turned around, and looked at me and although her mouth did not say the words, her eyes did: "Child, if only you knew how much I understand but cannot respond to."

I couldn't wait for speech lessons to begin. Arrangements were made for a therapist to come to the house and we decided that the cherry wood oval table in the dining room was the best place to hold the sessions.

On a Wednesday afternoon a couple of weeks after her release from the hospital came the first lesson and we seated ourselves at the table with considerable expectation. How much progress had she made in her understanding? I sat near Tante Corrie so that I could translate the therapist's directions into Dutch. In order to evaluate how much Tante Corrie could comprehend, the therapist first took some straight pieces of plastic.

"Make a square of this please," she said.

Tante Corrie looked at me and winked and formed the pieces of plastic into a square.

Next came six wooden blocks with the letters of her name out of sequence.

"Will you spell Corrie for me?" she asked slowly.

Tante Corrie put C, O, and R in the correct order, after which her efforts seemed tired and confused. Next she was asked to copy lines, circles, and a stick figure.

After a few more exercises the first session came to a close. I was shocked by the degree to which her comprehension was diminished, but if Tante Corrie realized the extent of her disability it did not show on her face.

Speech lessons were to take place twice a week from then on. Her therapist would be coming again on Friday.

The next day Tante Corrie decided that it would be nice to take a walk. She indicated that by walking to the hall closet where her coat was kept, and pointing at the front door. She took my arm and we went outside.

As we stepped from the pavement to cross the road, making in the direction of the park, I recalled the conversation she and I had had when we walked in that exact area a few months before. Then she had said, "We will be together until the end. Or rather, until the wonderful new beginning."

"Yes, we will," I replied, never realizing what that commitment was to mean. But a promise was a promise.

I thought, *I would have thought that she needed a good nurse, not an impractical person like me.*

Yet there was nothing else to be done but to continue down the road that was set before us. It was the beginning of October, five weeks after the stroke, and we were walking in the sunshine to Bradford Park. Emotionally we were on a roller coaster of a road that kept bringing new obstacles to overcome. Spiritually we were on a highway of faith that neither of us had ever been on before.

Friday came, and Tante Corrie seated herself at the oval table several minutes before the therapist even arrived. This time the therapist took cards three inches high with colored pictures and laid two of them in front of Tante Corrie.

"Show me the ball."

Tante Corrie's finger found the right card.

"Now show me the dog."

She was able to identify it.

After practicing for a while with two cards, the therapist graduated to three, then four. Usually Tante Corrie could identify the pictures.

Quite pleased with the afternoon's work, the teacher left saying that she would be back the next week and gave us a set of cards so that we could do homework sessions.

At least twice a day Tante Corrie took my hand and led me to the oval table. I took the cards and laid them before her, not too many at a time, as I had seen the therapist do.

Tante Corrie did her homework with the drive and enthusiasm I had seen her employ when she was well. She was doing all she could to hasten the day when speech and reading and writing would return, and we rejoiced together at any small improvement.

One day she was tired and a little depressed. I laid out the cards at our homework session, starting with just four. By then, we had had several sessions with the speech therapist, who was using six.

"Where is the book, Tante Corrie?"

She hesitated and pointed to the pen.

"No, that is not right, but they are related. You write in a book with a pen."

"Can you show me the book now?"

She studied the cards carefully but could not identify the book. We tried again with different subjects on new cards.

"Which is the lamp?"

She pointed to the correct card.

"Yes! Now, where is the knife?"

She searched for it in vain.

My respect for her grew deeper with the passing days. It would have been so easy just to give up. She never did. She did her homework faithfully and was always eager to start when the therapist arrived. I thought that even if this accomplished little else, at least she was receiving some mental stimulation and had a plan and a goal. How she had always loved plans. I just could not imagine how Corrie ten Boom could live without a plan.

We continued to pray that God would give her back her speech and asked Him to help us communicate. We were learning fast. We had lived together for two and a half years and so knew each other well enough to meet certain needs. And the long periods of silence were not particularly irksome. I was discovering that there can be remarkable communication in silence.

For instance, I might be thinking about the Scripture we had just read, or the matter I had just explained, or be trying to puzzle out what she had just wanted to know, or would be praying for the answer, when suddenly the Lord would bring into my mind the answer to her question or I would know that which she had wanted to convey. I saw her face light up again and again as her needs were met. The communication system was a combination of many factors—the obtaining of as much information as possible on this condition called "aphasia," the fact that two people very much wanted to communicate, the daily reading of the Bible, much prayer together, and an increasing desire to be made aware of each other's needs. We needed to watch each other's expressions, keep to as strict a routine as possible so that a minimum of confusion was caused, and simply be quiet.

Tante Corrie's understanding was definitely improving. If a matter was explained slowly and simply in Dutch she would usually comprehend. The baffling thing was, though, that she would not always comprehend, even if it were a subject she had understood before.

When the time came for Tante Corrie's next checkup at the doctor's office he was pleased with her physical progress. There had been no regaining of the lost weight, but she was eating well and I was able to tell him that the throat muscles had improved in strength and that she could eat normally now. She walked with no difficulty, could use her right hand, and no longer needed help and company at night. The doctor had received a report from the speech therapist who told him that Tante Corrie's comprehension had improved so much that she thought she would benefit from lessons at the Speech and Rehabilitation Department of a large hospital in nearby Fullerton. Her specialist encouraged Tante Corrie to continue lessons: "It will mean more hard work," he said, "but you are used to that." Tante Corrie accepted the idea with enthusiasm.

When arrangements were made, we discovered it meant attending lessons four times a week. Surely it could not be much longer before her speech returned. The journeys to

Fullerton began in November, two and a half months after the stroke.

On the first day we joined other stroke patients and people with speech problems in the waiting room of the Speech Department. Their ages ranged from about ten years, a friendly mongoloid boy, to Tante Corrie's eighty-six and at once there was a comradeship. There was a certain relief in finding that there were others with similar problems.

After a short wait, a slim young woman with curly brown hair and large gray eyes came and introduced herself as Janice. She was kind and reassuring, and when the first session came to a close she told me privately, "At the end of each month I am going to test Corrie. If the test shows that there has been no improvement over the last month, there will be no point in continuing with lessons. We know through experience that if no improvement is shown by the test, any further return of functional speech or communication is unlikely."

Four times a week we traveled to the hospital in Fullerton and Tante Corrie applied all her strength to doing the best she could at her lessons. It paid off for when Janice performed the test at the end of the first month there was a definite improvement.

No functional speech was yet forthcoming, yet Tante Corrie made the best of it. Attempting to communicate was creative and she had always been good at that.

One day we sat on the patio under the hummingbird feeder and I tried to teach her to pronounce my name: "Tante Corrie, say *P*," I said, slowly pronouncing the consonant.

She copied the sound.

"Now *A*." She pronounced it like an *E* as most Dutch people do.

"And *M*." She did so.

"Now you have got three sounds. Watch my mouth and see if you can say *Pam*."

Tante Corrie looked at me closely.

After a short silence a word came: "Map." She had done her best, but had gotten the word backward.

For a moment, I thought she might retreat into discouragement. Instead Tante Corrie burst into laughter. She could hear that it was wrong, but could do nothing about it.

The visits to the hospital continued. Four times a week we greeted our quiet new acquaintances in the waiting area before Tante Corrie was admitted to Janice's room.

And we persevered at home. Tante Corrie was able to tolerate more now and even enjoy a little television in the evenings. This showed me that things were making more sense to her.

The end of the second month arrived, and again Janice's test showed an improvement.

Most of all, I was amazed that Tante Corrie's love for people did not lessen, despite her own difficulties. We sat outside with a cup of coffee one sunny day, when the vines had lost their leaves for the winter but the garden was green and pleasant. That day, however, her attention was not given to the citrus trees or the birds. Taking a final sip, she put her coffee cup down firmly on the patio table, closed her eyes and prayed, using words that were not intelligible to me, and not prayer in the spirit, for she often tried to speak in the way she was praying then. With a clear "Amen," she looked at me quizzically and pointed at me with her finger. I thought we were probably about to embark on a journey of discovery. Sure enough, we set off.

"Do you want something, Tante Corrie?"

"No."

"Are you thinking about a person?"

"Yes."

"Is it a man?"

"No."

"A woman then. Is she married?"

"Yes."

"Is she a mother?"

"Yes."

"Has she got three children?"

"No."

"Two children?"

"Yes."

Through a long process of elimination we finally arrived at the person—one of tens of thousands of acquaintances—whom Tante Corrie was thinking about. She was thrilled when the correct name was called out. We had taken perhaps three-quarters of an hour to arrive at the answer to a question that under normal circumstances could have been stated in a few seconds. Tante Corrie made me tell all I knew about recent events in that lady's life, and she immediately prayed for her.

Why should that person have been placed on Tante Corrie's heart? I wrote her a letter. By return post she replied.

"Dear Corrie, Now I know for sure that God is interested in both the little and big problems in our lives. The fact that He put us on your heart and that you have prayed for us is a great encouragement. . . ." She went on to explain the crisis that was taking place in her family at the time. Tante Corrie was so happy that the Lord had used her. Prayer was vital and she had not only prayed, she had shown enough concern and love to want to spend a very tiring forty-five minutes in order to find out about the woman and her family. Her life was not useless.

The time came around for the next test at the Speech Department. Two days after that, Janice ushered us into her room at the hospital and we went through the usual routine.

Janice seemed a bit dispirited, I thought. At the end of the session she broke the news gently: "Corrie, your test did not show any improvement this month. That means that after the end of this month we will stop having speech lessons. It will be good for you, though, to keep practicing at home."

Tante Corrie listened and nodded with no show of emotion. Had she really understood Janice's words and what they meant?

We walked slowly out of the hospital into the clear, cool winter afternoon, her hand through my right arm, and made our way to the parked car. I talked to her about things that we saw on the way home and she responded as usual with her *Ja* when appropriate.

On our return to Shalom House she rested for a few minutes while I prepared a sandwich for supper. As we sat at the oval table she pointed toward the sitting room.

"Do you mean the television, Tante Corrie? This is the night when we like to look at the lovely nature program."

"Ja!"

Still no sign that she had been given the news that she would in all probability never speak again.

We sat together later that evening watching the program, and when it was over and I had turned the television off there was silence for a few minutes. All I could hear was the ticking of the little brown clock.

"Tante Corrie," I said, "I am just going to the kitchen to make some warm milk for us and we will have a couple of those new shortbread cookies."

I walked back to the kitchen, turned on the gas, and heated some milk, pouring it into two china cups with a flower pattern, then placing a couple of shortbread cookies on each saucer. The cups were rather overfull.

Moving slowly from the kitchen back to the sitting room I passed the oval table where so many hours had been spent recently at speech lessons and homework. Walking carefully on, my eyes on the overfull cups, I entered the sitting room.

Coming to a stop in front of the white sofa where she was sitting I was just about to say, "Here you are, Tante Corrie," when I looked up and saw something I had never witnessed before.

Corrie ten Boom was weeping openly.

9.

A Time to Be Silent

In December of 1978, Lotte Reimeringer became part of our household. She and Tante Corrie had known each other for more than thirty years and her arrival was a great joy. During her visit to the United States the previous summer when she had been part of the tribute, "This Is Your Life," Lotte was asked to consider returning to help with the new daily devotional book, *This Day Is the Lord's,* Tante Corrie's sixth book since coming to Shalom House.

Now there was much more reason for her to come. Since Tante Corrie's stroke it had become increasingly clear that she needed more than one full-time helper. Elizabeth worked only part-time, and though the many volunteers were invaluable, her condition demanded continuous assistance and companionship. Lotte was not a trained nurse, but had had a good deal of practice at nursing over many years. She was also an excellent housekeeper and secretary. So Lotte moved into Shalom House's guest room. She set to work as soon as possible to help complete the daily devotional book, about one-third of which had already been written by Tante Corrie prior to the stroke and typed out by me.

During her many years of travel, Corrie ten Boom had always kept a notebook handy. One of the things that had greatly impressed me when I first met her was her desire to get to know and serve the Lord Jesus better. She was willing to learn from old and young, rich and poor, intellectual and uneducated. Once, while attending a funeral with her in

Holland, I saw her making copious notes of the message that a young evangelist was giving. She had collected many thousands of notes, statements, and anecdotes and particularly liked to write down short statements or catchy phrases that she called "clippings."

Searching for material for the devotional book, Lotte went through the notebooks with Tante Corrie, and together they decided which of the notes should be included. Tante Corrie was very much involved again in her project, and we prayed the prayer I had often heard her say: "Lord, will You let every word be written that should be written, and will You prevent every word from being written that should not be written?"

Yet another chapter in life in Shalom House was evolving and I found myself having to deal with a new element in my life—the need for long-term patience. Tante Corrie's diminished state had been going on for several months and I had no way of knowing how long it would continue. I could see it was going to be necessary to ask God continually for all that I needed to stay the course. It was one thing to be faithful in a crisis, but I needed to learn to be faithful in the long haul.

I had many a difficult struggle in my mind as we moved to the end of 1978, but discovered that each time I surrendered my will to the will of God, He gave me peace or strength or whatever I needed to continue. I began to think that perhaps in His great love there was no other way of keeping me close to Him, but to allow me to come into this situation where I had to learn to rely on Him completely.

Lotte and I tried to arrange a routine that would allow Tante Corrie the necessary rest and yet give her sufficient activity.

In a way, the work went on as usual. Elizabeth continued to keep house for us. Tante Corrie's publisher sent the galley proofs for the books that she had written before her illness, her board members and office staff kept in touch with her.

One evening five months after the stroke we were sitting on the white sofa when Tante Corrie pointed at me with her left index finger.

"Do you want something to eat?"

"No."

"Would you like to go to bed now?"

I exhausted all the usual questions but could not hit on the subject she needed to know about. Instead of being upset, Tante Corrie gave a little shrug of her shoulders as if to say, "You are sure to think of it sooner or later." We changed the subject, while I read to her from the mail that had arrived that day. Later in the evening I thought back to our sessions on the white sofa before she became ill and how we had sewed together. "Tante Corrie," I said, "do you mean that you would like to try your needlework?"

"Ja!" she said triumphantly.

So that was it. I had thought it would be too complicated for her to follow a pattern. And though it took a little while for her still slightly weak right hand to adjust to holding the needle, she soon mastered it. Daily, she began working on the cushion cover she had started months before.

As the weeks progressed, I saw that a pattern was emerging. And I thought of the way I used to make long, detailed lists of "things to do today," and how I so enjoyed an ordered schedule. Now such a schedule was absolutely necessary—and, it occurred to me that God had certainly known this when He had brought me together with Tante Corrie.

Lotte and I made sure that Tante Corrie had a daily walk, for she loved fresh air and sunshine. There was no sign of the original right-sided paralysis. We also took several car trips with our silent charge. She liked being driven to a certain hillside to watch the colors change on the snowy mountains to the east as the sun set behind us. We took picnics to the oceanside where she enjoyed the fresh sea breezes and all the color—the deep blue of the ocean and the sky, the red, orange, and yellow of the semitropical flowers and shrubs, the gracious palm trees.

I wonder what Tante Corrie's memory is like now, I thought as the three of us watched seagulls circling overhead one sunny afternoon. She had always loved birds. It reminded me of a story she often told about the concentration camp.

She and thousands of other women had been forced to attend roll call, which officially began at 4:30 a.m. but to which they were often called earlier by the Germans in an effort to break their morale. The nights were cold and black, and the prisoners were being guarded by people who had had, as she often said, "a training in cruelty." There were moments of great despair. One dark morning, as she stood in rank with thousands of other women, all stamping their feet to keep warm, her heart felt desolate and it seemed that God had forgotten her and Betsie. Suddenly, high above them, a skylark began to sing. And as she looked up she was reminded of Psalm 103, "As high as the heavens are above the earth, so great is his love for those who fear him. . . ." Immediately she was lifted in her spirit above the misery of her circumstances and knew that God had not forgotten her.

As we watched the seagull circling against the deep blue sky, I wondered whether she was thinking of the skylark. There was freedom all around her and nobody was treating her cruelly, yet this was a kind of imprisonment.

"Tante Corrie, do you remember the skylark?"

"Ja!" She beamed at me with sparkling blue eyes. There was nothing wrong with her memory. How glad I was that we had spent so many evenings with our needlework while she told stories of events that had taken place throughout her long life. I hoped that I could remember many of them so that we could have communication in this way.

One way in which life continued as usual at Shalom House was the frequent receiving of visitors. In this way Tante Corrie was kept in touch with the outside world. Lotte and I explained who was coming and reminded her of facts about them. If more than one visitor was present we asked that just one person speak at a time, explaining to them that it was very tiring for Tante Corrie if she had to try to follow two conversations at once. Sitting close to Tante Corrie with the guest opposite her so that she could see him or her clearly, one of us translated for her that which the guest was saying if she had not been able to catch it in English. We watched her reactions very carefully to try to pick up that which she might be wanting to communicate to them. We asked questions on her behalf, knowing the kinds of things she liked to ask because we had been with her during many similar visits when she was well.

"Tell me what the Lord has been doing in your lives lately."

"Tell me about your children."

Tante Corrie received the visitors in a relaxed way, and we explained to them in her presence that she had had a stroke and that was why she could not speak to them as she would want to. Her outgoing interest in and love for people had not diminished in spite of her severe handicap, but some visitors found it awkward to hold a basically one-sided conversation. Others were very gifted at it. What *was* the key to good communication by visitors?

From the point of view of natural gifts, those people whose work involved them in communication, for example actors, journalists, or teachers, could often gain contact with her more easily than others. But those who gained the best contact of all were those who had prayerfully prepared for their visit with her and had asked God for a word of encouragement or a way of meeting her needs. These people were not embarrassed or self-conscious.

At practically every visit I wished that the guest did not find it necessary to fill times of silence with animated conversation, but I sympathized, too. I myself had only recently learned that there could be communication and fellowship simply in sitting quietly in somebody's presence.

There were not enough hours in the day to try to accommodate the number of visitors who wanted to come, and the sessions were tiring. After about half an hour, usually, Tante Corrie closed her eyes and began to pray. Her mind knew what she wanted to pray, but her lips could not form the words. Nevertheless, she made sounds anyway, ending the prayer with a clear "Hallelujah, Amen," leaving the visitor in no doubt that it was time to leave.

A question I asked myself was how Tante Corrie would react if she had to meet people for whom she was totally unprepared.

One day when Lotte had been with us for three months, we decided to take a picnic to the seaside again and found a shady spot under the palm trees where we set up our deck chairs and spread out a little cloth on the grass.

Suddenly I saw that two ladies and a gentleman were approaching us and they looked very Dutch. They obviously recognized her but probably did not know about her present condition.

Oh, dear, I thought, *I don't think she knows these people, and we do not even have the advantage of gaining a little time for her in which to understand because it won't be necessary to translate for her.*

Sure enough, one lady extended her hand, smiling, and said: *"Bent U Corrie ten Boom?"*

"Ja," she said.

We explained to the people, visitors from Holland, what had happened to Tante Corrie. To my relief she smiled and communicated with them, not through words but through the love God gave her for people There was absolutely no embarrassment.

Come to think of it, I mused as we drove home, *I have never seen Tante Corrie embarrassed. She always expected that people would take her just as she was. And now, after her stroke she still expects it.* It was the result of a deep confidence that God accepted her just as she was and it had not been shaken now that she could not speak. She was accepted, and so she could accept people just as they were.

The receiving of visitors and our little excursions took a fair amount of time, yet there was still quite a large part of the day to be filled. I began to study her book, *A Prisoner and Yet* . . . to find out how Tante Corrie spent her days in solitary confinement in 1944:

It was oppressively quiet in the prison. The time dragged slowly by. So unlike former days! I always had been so very busy. There was never a moment in the day when I was not doing something. And now . . . ! However, my days of imprisonment would not be over until I had served my time; and my one purpose therefore had to be to pass away the time, somehow. A colorful bath towel had been sent to me from home. I unraveled it and used the colored threads to embroider all my clothes. On my pajama top I conjured a window with curtains, a cyclamen, a cat and butterflies. I kept adding to it until my pajamas were like a colorful print. It was a delightful diversion, and the days passed not too slowly. When singing, I laid aside my embroidery work; it would have been an extravagance to do two things at the same time.

Thirty-five years later, at Shalom House in Placentia, it was also an extravagance to do two things at the same time. And not just an extravagance, it simply was not possible. Tante Corrie, like so many stroke patients, became extremely tired if her attention had to be divided. Not only did we try to ensure that we never had two conversations going on in a room at the same time, because of the difficulty this caused her in hearing and understanding, we also discovered that it was fatiguing to have any background noise to a conversation or activity. Therefore, when we listened to music, we did only that. How she loved Bach. We listened for lengths of time usually not exceeding thirty minutes and I sometimes said to her: "Tante Corrie, are you thinking about heaven? Do you remember how you told us that we can never use our imaginations too strongly? You said, 'The Bible tells us that no eye has seen or ear has heard, neither has it even come into man's heart the things that God has prepared for those who love Him. Therefore when I use my imagination I know that the reality will be a trillion times better than anything I can think of. But in my imagination I am singing in the angelic choirs and the choirs are being conducted by Bach himself.' "

She nodded and smiled.

Taking one activity at a time, we spent our days. Bible reading and prayer, work on the daily devotional book, meals taken slowly, coffee and tea breaks, music, walks, drives, needlework, all at a slow rate, visitors, rest times, and in between it all, much communication without words.

We learned to treasure small experiences and make the most of them. Long minutes were spent watching the hummingbird flashing iridescent green and red, its speed and energy in such marked contrast to that of its silent observer. We savored the taste of our coffee and the piece of dark chocolate. We walked slowly around the garden paying attention to the flowers. We felt the silk of the rose petals. We studied the translucent pink of a particular bloom. We bent down and smelled its sweet scent.

Now and then, very surprisingly, Tante Corrie was able to speak a few words in answer to a question.

I had a question one day nearly six months after the stroke that I hesitated putting to her. Having been born in the last century, she did not like it when ladies wore pants. She and I never discussed the matter in particular when it came to my clothes, but I knew that she preferred me not to wear them so I usually did not. This morning, however, as I looked at the contents of my wardrobe, I decided that I had nothing to wear except a blouse and pants.

"Would you mind if I wore pants today?" I asked her, expecting a shake or a nod of the head.

Instead she said clearly in Dutch: "Whatever do you want to do that for?"

"Well," I said, amazed by this definite reply, "I don't seem to be able to find anything else to wear."

"Nonsense!" came the reply again.

Although you always knew where you stood with Tante Corrie, it was not really typical of her to be that blunt. She, Lotte, and I laughed a lot about it. She had not meant to be unkind, but had used a word that happened to come to her mind. I found a skirt to wear that day instead.

The days and weeks went slowly by. Sometimes I watched her while she sat in the garden and it would seem that she was withdrawn. I would have given a lot to know what she was thinking.

In all this, we tried to understand what God was doing, what He was saying through Tante Corrie's present condition.

Tante Corrie went to bed fairly early, and on several occasions when the day's activities were over and the phone had stopped ringing, Lotte and I sat on the white sofa and talked about her suffering. We prayed for insight and understanding. We took our Bibles and searched for what God had to say on the subject. The verse that struck us most strongly was this one: ". . . If indeed we share in his sufferings in order that we may also share in his glory" (Rom. 8:17).

I told Lotte about the time a few months prior to her stroke when Tante Corrie came to my room late one night very excited after talking to the Lord and asking that she might see some of His glory. He had assured her that she would. Was this part of His answer to that prayer?

We began to see that suffering and glory were strongly related in the Bible and in the lives of Christians through the centuries. We also remembered the statement Tante Corrie had made while in solitary confinement: "My days of imprisonment will not be over until I have served my time."

Now, years later, she was serving time again in another kind of imprisonment and the serving of the time was related to the question of seeing His glory. Had the Lord allowed her to come into this state of silence, helplessness, and utter dependence on Himself in order to show her more of His glory? We became more sensitive to watch for God's handiwork in this suffering, wondering how this seemingly endless situation was going to work out in conformity with His nature of goodness and love. We thought of Tante Corrie's attitude. It was saying to us that although she did not like to suffer, seeing it had come to her, she was not fighting it. She was accepting it, believing that somehow He was going to turn it into freedom and glory in His time. Could it be that this mysterious time in her life was not only for her own sake, but for the sake of the people immediately around her and of those to whom she was reaching out?

During coffee time in the sitting room one day, Tante Corrie pointed to one of the walls above the white sofa. We asked her if she would like us to rearrange the small prints of Dutch masters hanging there. No, that was not her desire. Shall we move them from the wall? Yes. Do you want others in their place? No. Do you want just one in their place? Ja! Which one? We three looked at each other in silence for a moment. Tante Corrie pointed toward the door. Shall we buy a new picture? No. Wait a moment, do you perhaps want a picture from Holland? Ja. Anticipation lit up her face. Tante Corrie—the portrait of your father? Ja!

As soon as possible, arrangements were made for its transportation, and Casper ten Boom's portrait was placed where Tante Corrie indicated she wanted it hung. It was somehow reassuring to have this painting in the house. It belonged here.

Now, partly because we had more time, but mainly because our circumstances forced us to lean on it, the Word of God was more precious to us than ever. We read to Tante Corrie often and noticed repeatedly that although there were days when she was very tired and normal conversation was confusing, the Bible always made sense. Never did we see a perplexed look when we read the Bible to her. Of special encouragement were several verses.

"Be strong and take heart and wait for the Lord."

"I have loved you with an everlasting love."

"My God will meet all your needs according to His glorious riches in Christ Jesus."

We read the Bible slowly. We meditated on it and relished its words.

The reading of books was another activity that brought enjoyment to our stroke patient. For her it was a richer pastime than is usually the case because Tante Corrie had her own works read back to her. Lotte read nearly all the approximately twenty books that she had written and Tante Corrie looked forward to the sessions eagerly when she relived some of the adventures from her past when the Lord had worked on her behalf in many a difficult situation. There is no doubt that she was greatly built up in her faith through her own testimony.

As a result of reading her books we talked about her two previous companions often. Connie worked with Tante Corrie from 1960 to 1967 and part of their life and travels together were recounted in *Tramp for the Lord*. It was a joy to her to be reminded about Connie who died of cancer not long after her marriage in 1967. She had evidently been a very vivacious person with a wonderful sense of humor, and it is a tribute to her memory that the only name Tante Corrie could now call out when she needed somebody was "Connie!" meaning that she needed the help represented in that name.

We talked a lot about Ellen, too. Ellen was happy in her new calling as wife and mother. She telephoned and wrote often and sent lots of photographs.

We looked forward to the daily arrival of the mail and she was always particularly glad to hear from her nephews and nieces, her late sister Nollie's children who lived in The Netherlands, Switzerland, and New Zealand, and from the many old "club girls" whom she had known years ago in Haarlem. On hearing their recounting of events of sixty or seventy years ago her face would light up as if it had happened yesterday.

Hundreds of letters came to Tante Corrie as a result of her films and books. In fulfillment of God's promise when He gave her Shalom House, it seemed that more people than ever were being touched by her message on film and in books.

An example of the many letters is this one:

"What Jesus has brought you through has been a constant encouragement to me. Often during times of deep suffering our Comforter has brought me scenes of your walk with Him. I read *The Hiding Place* with tears of joy, then went to see the movie. A non-Christian went with us and the next day she received Christ."

Much love and kindness were shown by both distant and local friends and neighbors who sent gifts of flowers and stopped by with fruit, vegetables, and cookies.

The prayer meeting for prisoners was held each week at

our neighbors' home, and whenever possible Tante Corrie was present, listening, and praying with her own language of unrelated sounds. She was very matter-of-fact about the situation. It was the best she could do, and after all, God understood.

If the stroke had impaired her physical senses, it evidently had little effect on her amazingly discerning spirit. This I learned in an incident with one of our visitors.

People continued to arrive in droves at Shalom House, and it happened several times that people called to say that they had been directed by the Lord to come and see Corrie. This was a bit disconcerting. If the Lord had told the caller to do something, who was I to argue with that? Sometimes I knew they were right, but sometimes I was sure they were not right. Even so, I let them come anyway, with the result that Tante Corrie became very overtired. As time went on I became bolder in not allowing certain visits.

That led to a disagreement with one would-be visitor who was convinced that the Lord had told her she must visit Tante Corrie. I knew Tante Corrie was very tired, and seeing the Lord had not told me the same thing, I did not allow the woman to come. Misunderstanding resulted, which strained the relationship. And although I tried to hide it from Tante Corrie, she was not deceived.

Her blue eyes seemed to look into my soul, and she tried to tell me something. Knowing what she probably meant, I helped her: "Tante Corrie, do you mean that disagreement I am having with Mrs. ——?"

"Ja!" she nodded triumphantly.

"Do you want me to get in touch with her and to put things right between her and me?"

"Ja!"

As soon as we could, the lady and I met to talk, pray, and put the matter in order. I began to see that Tante

Corrie's peace of mind and that of the other members of the household depended in part on maintaining good relationships with the many people who influenced our lives from outside our home.

As we tried to keep these "short accounts" with each other and with outside acquaintances, visitors to Shalom House remarked on its peacefulness and on Tante Corrie's inner tranquility. There was a radiance about her that was very beautiful and it came from the Lord. Lotte and I were sure that there was a deep communion going on between her and her Master. We longed to know what He was saying to her. Would we ever know?

Another of the subjects Lotte and I discussed during our quiet evenings on the white sofa under the portrait of Father ten Boom was why God had allowed this illness to take place. We wondered, talked, and prayed on the subject, but never came up with a complete answer to the mystery. We felt there was a lot we did not understand about why God allows suffering. What came to us in increasing measure was an assurance of the absolute sovereignty of God. He allowed suffering, and in His sovereignty, this time in Tante Corrie's life had also been ordained.

Why both were so, or how it was possible that both could be so, we did not know. But we concluded that both the allowing and the ordaining were part of the loving plan of God. Along with the awareness of His sovereignty came a fresh and new consciousness of His love. Never before had the love of God been so consistently real to me.

The question *why* was also put to us by many visitors. But Lotte and I soon stopped asking it, the reason being that Tante Corrie never did. There was no indication that she had a struggle with the question. Her attitude was one of acceptance. God had shut her up with Himself in a kind of precious imprisonment, and, so far, what was going on in her spirit was a secret between the two of them.

A way of encouraging Tante Corrie was to talk about the glorious future awaiting her in heaven. We read to her what the Bible has to tell us about it—there will be no sorrow, but an abiding joy, there will be a place prepared by the Lord, there will be service in heaven, and we will be forever with the Lord.

Sometimes Tante Corrie raised her hands to God as we talked about heaven with a look of great longing on her face. If it had depended on her will, she would have gone to be with Christ. It did not depend on her will, however, but on His. She was on earth still for one reason. It was the will of God, and something had yet to be accomplished within that will.

Of vital importance to me was the growing realization that our times were completely in God's hands. He knew the length of Tante Corrie's life. It did not depend on anything except His will. We often read to her and to ourselves what the Bible says about the length of life: "All the days ordained for me were written in your book before one of them came to be" (Ps. 139:16).

Tante Corrie had not been able to speak for months, and as I looked at her acceptance of her trials, my own smaller problems seemed to pale into far less significance. Seeing her patience I remembered her words: "Pam, you have got to learn to see great things great and small things small." As I thought of these things daily in the light of a new and awesome awareness of God's sovereignty, I found that I was beginning to learn to look more and more in the right direction, and as I did so, I started to see things in a more correct perspective.

A regular part of life was the stand that it was necessary to take against the attacks of the devil. Tante Corrie went through some dark moments when she was confused and downhearted. One such moment occurred in the spring seven months after her stroke. She became agitated, and Lotte and I tried to calm her. Human effort was not sufficient. She remained upset.

"Corrie," said Lotte, "I believe that this is an attack of the enemy. He would try to take away your joy. Let's pray."

Tante Corrie consented immediately.

"Father," prayed Lotte, "we come to You in the mighty name of Jesus Christ and we take authority over the devil who is trying to confuse and frighten Corrie. We resist him in Jesus' name and we pray that in the place of confusion You will bring Your peace and comfort. Thank You, Father. Amen."

At once Tante Corrie calmed down and her tranquility was restored. It was one of many similar instances during those months.

On Easter Day of 1979, eight months after her stroke, Tante Corrie celebrated her eighty-seventh birthday. There was an extra reason for celebration, because the daily devotional book *This Day Is the Lord's* had now been completed by her and Lotte.

Tante Corrie's eyes had been troubling her and we prayed that the Lord would give her relief from this discomfort. Judging by her attempt to describe the symptoms, she could not see clearly and they were hurting her.

Nevertheless, it was a joyful birthday. We spent much of it outside in the sunshine. Lotte and I bought her a new dress and jacket, white with a small pattern in red, blue, and green, which she at once put on. We read Psalm 103 as was the custom in hers and many other Dutch households on the occasion of a birthday. Also in Dutch tradition we offered coffee and cream cakes to the guests. We moved the patio table and chairs over to Tante Corrie's orange tree. It could now be called a real tree with healthy, shining, dark green foliage, and had borne some fruit that we could not wait to see ripen.

There were lots of parcels that day—new pajamas, tablecloth and napkins, china cup and saucer, glass goblets, and an illustrated book about Israel.

After all the guests had gone home and we had returned to the sitting room, Tante Corrie turned on the television and pointed to it excitedly. It was not a channel or a subject that she usually watched. I thought her excitement meant that she knew of something interesting that was coming on and asked her whether I should change channels. No, that was not the answer. Whichever channel I turned to she still pointed excitedly. Finally she walked up to the screen and touched it, then turned to me and smiled.

"Oh, Tante Corrie, do you mean that you can see it properly? Has the Lord healed your eyes?"

"Ja!"

I prepared for bed that night going over the events in this traumatic yet strangely blessed past year of her life.

What would her new year bring to her? Would her work be completed this year?

Only God knew. And He was completely silent on the subject.

10.

A Holy Stirring in the Stillness

Throughout the spring of 1979, Tante Corrie continued to make the best of the situation, feeling apparently fairly healthy. Then, in May, she had a digestive disturbance, and her doctor arranged to have her admitted to the hospital for tests. As we packed her small suitcase at Shalom House ready for admission, Lotte said to her, "Who knows, perhaps you will be able to come home very soon."

Her reply was a radiant smile, a pointing upward with her right index finger and the words: "Yes . . . or . . ."

At the hospital, we were in for a small surprise. A nurse handed her a clipboard and a pen, asking her to sign a certain permission form. We told the nurse that Tante Corrie had not been able to sign her name in the nine months since her stroke, and that we would explain in Dutch the place on the paper where she could put a cross instead of a true signature. Before we could get the words out, Tante Corrie took the clipboard and pen and signed, "Corrie ten Boom," very clearly in the correct place. Why she was able to do it then and not at any other time we would never know, but it made her very happy.

Two days later, all tests having proved negative, she was discharged from the hospital. And having received advice on diet, we drove her back to Shalom House. Her mood was pensive, and Lotte and I concluded that she was a bit disappointed that she had not gone to heaven.

A few days later we three were going through the regular

morning routine. After breakfast and prayer, I went with Tante Corrie to help her get dressed. Suddenly she hesitated and began to fumble with her clothes. Her eyes glazed. As I helped her sit down, her body sagged toward the right and I realized another serious stroke was taking place. Lotte was at the other end of the house, unable to hear me, so I half-dragged Tante Corrie to her bed, feeling, as I did so, that once again strength was leaving the right side of her body. As I passed the door to the corridor I called out for Lotte. She came running from the kitchen and together we put Tante Corrie back to bed. I rushed to the phone to call the doctor. After what seemed an hour, but was in fact just a few minutes, he arrived at the house, examined Tante Corrie, and confirmed that she had had another stroke. She was beginning to lose consciousness and the doctor decided that, if possible, she should be cared for at home. We were only too willing for this, knowing it would be her desire to die in her own bed, should this be the Lord's time for her.

All day Lotte and I watched at her bedside. Her right side was limp and flaccid. At the times when she opened her eyes we talked to her but she was not able to respond. All that she had regained in terms of speech and communication appeared to have vanished that day and so again did the use of the right side of her body, although, as before, the left side was unaffected. We had now learned enough about strokes to know that we would have to wait several hours to see whether this stroke was going to affect her permanently. It could be that there had not been any further brain damage and that she would recover the use of her limbs as before, and also that she would regain communication to the level she had possessed it before this stroke. How we hoped.

After a while it was clear that the muscles on the right side of her throat were affected; she could not swallow without coughing or choking. We knew that this condition often righted itself in the couple of days after a stroke, but in her case it did not. To prevent dehydration an IV was introduced.

Caring for Tante Corrie in her own rather low bed became difficult and we decided that an electric bed would be a great help. I went to a local hospital equipment supply store and selected a fully automatic bed, which could be moved up and down so that we could adjust it to a practical nursing height, and had adjustable side rails. A delivery man came to set the bed up and while it had not looked so utilitarian in the large warehouse in which I had viewed it, its large size and iron sturdiness now seemed to dominate the room. It took a bit of getting used to. Tante Corrie's own bed with its carved headboard was removed from her room and put into storage in the garage. The main bedroom at the front of Shalom House turned into a hospital room.

At this time Sharon Lightfoot, our neighbor over the back fence, began to play an important role in our lives. A trained nurse, she did all she could to make Tante Corrie comfortable and to teach us how to look after her. She kept the IV going, and was ready to help day or night.

In those first days after this second stroke it looked very much as if Tante Corrie was going to be given her heart's desire and go to heaven. With Sharon's help, Lotte and I cared for her for three days and nights, after which time we knew we were going to need professional help at night. A night nurse was hired and she worked from 11 p.m. until 7 a.m., while Lotte and I took over daytime duty. Lotte was a very good nurse, by experience, not profession, extremely practical and disciplined, and had had a lot of practice in caring for seriously ill patients.

Tante Corrie remained paralyzed on her right side, could find no words, and was generally in a state of semiconsciousness or sleep. Elizabeth prepared nourishing liquid foods for her such as milk with egg and protein powder, and when Tante Corrie roused we tried to feed her this and other fluids through a syringe. It was easier for her swallow if it was cold. Her damaged throat could feel the cool liquid and deal with it better. She was able to take a very little at a time. Too much caused her to choke. Every time she showed signs of consciousness we put the syringe in her mouth. The IV ceased to function several times because of the weak state of her veins and had to be reintroduced. Bright light hurt her eyes, so we half-closed the drapes, and the days were spent in semi-darkness. As her illness progressed, extra help was needed and a nursing aide came to help us during the day.

Even when she was unconscious, Lotte and I sensed it was very important to read the Scriptures to Tante Corrie. One day we stood beside her bed in her half-darkened bedroom. She was lying on her right side, the hand into which the IV needle was inserted resting on a pillow. The head of the electric bed was slightly raised. Silver hair reached to her shoulders, her eyes were closed and she was dressed in a blue and white hospital-style gown tied with strings behind her neck. There was no reason, judging by her inert posture, to think that she could hear. But Lotte read anyway: "Find rest, O my soul in God alone; my hope comes from him."

We prayed with her and talked to her, explaining what had happened, which day it was, what time of day, who was in the room, and that she would not be left alone.

Tante Corrie did not remain totally uncommunicative. Three days after the stroke the expression in her eyes changed. It is not possible to say what she was feeling—only she knew that—but her eyes were not wide and staring, as in fear, or darting, as in anxiety. They were quiet and full of rest, and they left me quiet and full of rest. Even in this serious illness there was an inner tranquility that had not been disturbed. We knew it was the Lord's doing. For His own reasons He was allowing a further testing of her faith, and she was going through it with Him.

Ten days after the stroke, the IV having once again become ineffective, the decision was taken to move her to the hospital, where a more effective and permanent IV was inserted into the sub-clavian vein. This time she had her own room and we were able to be with her continuously, in shifts. We were thankful that there was a couch in the room on which we could rest. For a week she remained seriously ill. As with the previous stroke I saw the effect the trauma caused to her brain. There was irritation of the brain lining, causing restlessness. She ate very little and slept a great deal. After a few days she began to respond better when awake, but most medical advisors said she would not recover.

A week after her admission to the hospital, however, she turned a corner. It was late on a Sunday morning, and during the more than three hours when I had sat next to a sleeping Tante Corrie, I had read quite a bit of the Sunday edition of the *Los Angeles Times*. At around eleven, I looked over the top of the paper into two very awake blue eyes. She pushed back the sheet and moved her unparalyzed leg toward the edge of the bed. Hardly able to believe that she was fully conscious after two-and-a-half weeks, I asked her if she wanted to get up. She nodded. It was a great moment when I saw that some of her communicative faculties had returned. I went to the nurses' station and shortly afterward two nurses came to the room, one with a wheelchair. While one nurse held the IV and supported Tante Corrie's back, the other swiveled her into the wheelchair. She sat up for forty-five minutes, and ate quite well.

If I had thought that this degree of consciousness and desire to eat were to be maintained, I was wrong. Sometimes she was alert and ate a little, at other times she was uncommunicative. The vigil continued.

Scripture reading played an enormous role in our lives. We read it to Tante Corrie, to each other and to ourselves, and each day God gave us verses from the Bible to strengthen us and help us carry on.

"As for God, his way is perfect; the word of the Lord is flawless. He is a shield for all who take refuge in him" (Ps. 18:30).

We watched her suffering continue and saw her body become more frail. We felt totally helpless in giving her any real aid. But an extraordinary thing was happening. As we became more tired and were thrust on the Lord for all that we needed, we found ourselves becoming more deeply convinced than ever of the wisdom and kindness and love of God.

One day one of her board members called. He encouraged me, saying, "This time is going to be used by the Lord to show some of the mysteries of life and the mysteries of death."

What a mystery it was. I had often heard it said that when a person gives up their will to live, they die, and when they will to live, they live. I watched Tante Corrie apply her ever-strong will during the coming days as she became more conscious.

A male visitor came one day when she was awake and lying on her right side. A pillow was supporting her to prevent her rolling onto her back. The nurses had just completed the two-hourly turn to prevent bedsores and the IV was on the side she was facing.

The visitor looked into her wide blue eyes that showed she was particularly awake that afternoon. He sat quietly at her side for a few minutes, then said: "I would like to ask the Lord to bring this suffering to an end for you. May I do that?"

She nodded, did not close her eyes, but watched his mouth.

"Lord," he said, "I ask You to release Tante Corrie from the suffering she is now having to bear. She has had a long and blessed life and wants very much to be with You. Will You please take her to heaven . . . ?"

Tante Corrie's eyes were riveted on his face. She was understanding each word. The look in her eyes was urgent and she was nodding as hard as her weak state allowed. As her visitor finished his prayer she smiled radiantly. There was no doubt as to what her will was. Her desire was "to depart and to be with Christ which is far better." But her will was subjected to the sovereign will of God, and she was so in tune with that will that as the days progressed and her strength began to return she did not fight the fact that she was getting better. We knew this by her acquiescent attitude and cooperation with attempts to help her eat and to regain mobility.

The day came when a young physical therapist appeared in her room and told her that exercises were going to commence that day. She took hold of Tante Corrie's weakened right hand and asked her to push against her own hand to see if she could move it. Although it took tremendous effort, Tante Corrie tried her best. She pushed and pushed until she had succeeded in moving it a few inches. Even so, in contrast with the previous stroke, the paralyzed right side showed little improvement.

Gradually her understanding improved, and the day came when the specialist told us she could be discharged soon, even though she still needed the IV. When we broke the news to Tante Corrie she smiled and nodded, leaving us in no doubt that she was longing for Shalom House.

Lotte and I rented the necessary equipment in order to be able to look after her, and after three weeks in the hospital an ambulance transported her home. Once again the house was full of flowers, but the journey from the hospital was so tiring for her we were not sure she even noticed them. For the next eight weeks she went through a time of severe illness and weakness. She would appear to be getting stronger, then have a relapse. She wanted to be up as much as her strength would allow, and from the physical therapist who came regularly to exercise her right arm and leg, we learned how to transfer her from her bed to the wheelchair. She was glad when she could be in the fresh air among her roses. At times she let us know that by the relaxed expression on her face. At other times she was less expressive, and to be up was simply an exhausting chore.

One day we had transferred Tante Corrie to her wheelchair from her bed, propping her up with pillows, because of the muscle weakness and the paralysis. We were on our way, slowly, from the bedroom to the garden, when the front doorbell rang. On answering it, I discovered Jane Klassen, the wife of Tante Corrie's university professor handyman. She was a familiar visitor to Shalom House with gifts of cookies, fresh bread, and vegetables. This time Jane had brought lettuce, tomatoes, and oranges from her garden and was accompanied by her young daughter, Kelly. I asked them to wait for a moment and we wheeled Tante Corrie toward the front door. Jane told me later that when she was confronted by Tante Corrie in that state of extreme weakness, the main impression was her lack of false pride. She could not speak, could only blink, and bottles and tubes seemed to be attached everywhere, but when she saw her friend and her little blonde-haired daughter, her face lit up in a crooked smile of welcome. Even with a child, who would perhaps have been shocked at seeing such infirmity, Tante Corrie was natural and relaxed. This wheelchair and her attachments were part of her life, and even now she was not embarrassed.

From the time we brought Tante Corrie home from the hospital she had the help of a night nurse and during the first weeks we had nursing help during the day. When the IV ceased to function, the doctor decided against returning her to the hospital as she was able to take enough fluids to remain comfortable. After several weeks it became possible for Lotte and me, with Elizabeth doing the shopping, cooking, and helping with nursing procedures where needed, to take care of her on our own. She was totally helpless and a routine had to be worked out and kept to. When she was not in her wheelchair, she needed frequent turning in bed. Sharon, our neighbor and volunteer registered nurse gave lots of advice.

It was so important that bedsores not be allowed to develop. This entailed keeping her skin clean and well-massaged and moving her position frequently. We were advised to buy an "egg crate mattress" made of soft foam rubber about six inches thick, with indentations giving the top the appearance of an egg crate. This was placed on top of the regular mattress of the electric bed. It was not possible for Tante Corrie to turn by herself, and Lotte and I evolved a system that we believed was easiest for Tante Corrie although not all patients would find it suitable.

Over the egg crate mattress we placed a fitted sheet and then took a plain top sheet and folded it in a strip about two-and-a-half feet wide that we placed under Tante Corrie extending from just below her shoulder blades. Lotte and I took hold of this draw sheet firmly, as close to Tante Corrie's body as possible, counted to three so that we both moved at the same time and lifted her body about an inch upward so that we did not scrape her back on the bed. We then turned her, with the sheet, to the left or the right, as necessary. A pillow was placed at her back under the draw sheet and on top of the fitted sheet, to prevent her rolling backward. The procedure took place many times, day and night. She took it patiently. When she was on her right side it gave her the opportunity to help us. As soon as the turn was completed she took hold of the bedrail with her unparalyzed left hand and pulled herself as far over as she could. We placed the pillow at her back and then she relaxed against it.

I could not get over the attitude of this fragile soldier on her iron chariot of a bed.

The Book of Job spoke to me as never before. I could identify her suffering with his. Lotte and I talked about it during our evening sessions on the white sofa, when the night nurse was on duty. We remembered how God had allowed Satan to test Job, first by taking away nearly all he had. When Job did not blame God, Satan appeared before the Lord a second time.

God said: "Have you considered my servant Job? There is no one on earth like him; he is blameless and upright, a man who fears God and shuns evil. And he still maintains his integrity, though you incited me against him to ruin him without any reason."

"Skin for skin!" Satan replied. "A man will give all he has for his own life. But stretch out your hand and strike his flesh and bones, and he will surely curse you to your face."

The Lord replied: "Very well, then, he is in your hands; but you must spare his life" (Job 2:3–6).

The Bible tells us that Satan left God's presence and caused great physical affliction to come upon Job. Even after that, Job did not sin. He said: "Shall we accept good from God, and not trouble?" (Job 2:10).

As well as thinking a lot about Job, we remembered the prophet Ezekiel, who, as part of his calling, was required by God to lie on his left side for 390 days, and on his right side for forty days.

The Lord told him: "I will tie you up with ropes so that you cannot turn from one side to the other until you have finished the days of your siege" (Ezek. 4:8).

What an extraordinary calling. I had never taken real

note of those verses before. We did not make any kind of aesthetic connection between Ezekiel and Tante Corrie, but noted that the response of the prophet and the response of God's twentieth-century servant were the same—obedience, not rebellion. Ezekiel had a message to proclaim and he proclaimed it. We were equally sure that Tante Corrie had a message to proclaim and was proclaiming it, yet without words. Her very attitude was proclaiming, "When the very worst happens, the Lord Jesus remains the same." Her life was saying that if she could be joyful and peaceful in her circumstances, other people surely could be in their easier ones, provided they too had a relationship with the Lord Jesus.

Such was Tante Corrie's general decline during the long, hot summer of 1979, three months after her second stroke, that all details for her memorial service and burial were worked out. A grave plot and casket were purchased, and Lotte looked up some of Tante Corrie's favorite organ pieces by Bach with which to begin and end the service.

At the end of three months the medical verdict was "she is going into kidney failure, which is another step in the inevitable process." Her weight, according to Sharon's experienced estimation, was about eighty pounds. Then, after exactly three months, against all medical prediction and against all apparent logic, Tante Corrie turned another corner.

Incredibly, she began to improve dramatically. She began to eat and drink, to put on weight, and her powers of communication intensified. When we looked at the circumstances we did not understand. When we looked at the Bible we were convinced again that her life and the life of every human being are in the hands of God. He and only He determines the length of every life. It was not our place to question His timing because we did not know the details of

His plans for Tante Corrie. As we read: "Man's days are determined; you have decreed the number of his months and have set limits he cannot exceed" (Job 14:5).

We took stock of the circumstances. Tante Corrie's first stroke had rendered her mute, but she had regained her ability to walk. This second stroke had inflicted more brain damage. Her understanding was apparently less and she was unable to move without assistance. Yet God had allowed it, and we knew He would help her as He had always done. We did not know how, but we tried to live minute by minute, not looking to the future, but receiving grace just for the present moment.

At this time another encouragement that a person does not die until God's appointed time, came to us through the Bible's comment on King David:

". . . when David had served God's purpose in his own generation, he fell asleep . . ." (Acts 13:36).

Up until this time, in common with a large part of the western world, I had set great store by strength and achievement. A sense of satisfaction was gained by having a goal and employing all faculties, strength, and input from others in order to reach that goal. Particularly in America, I had found "self-image," or our view of ourselves, was related directly to what a person achieves. But what happens when a person becomes old, frail, brain-damaged, and in some eyes, apparently useless? How does God view that? How should society view that? I had been learning that our real selves can be discovered only in the Lord Jesus Christ. The Bible tells us that He loves us so much that He died to save us from our sins, that we are "precious, holy, beloved, dear children, hidden in the hollow of His hand." And in that hand He also holds our times.

Four months after the second stroke, American friends who had just visited Holland came to see Tante Corrie one day and brought her a gift. The opening of packages was a favorite occupation and she removed the ribbon and wrapping paper with her left hand and some help from us. Inside was a beautiful Delft blue china plate, with the words, in Dutch, *My times are in Your hands.*

We did not know whether she could decipher the words, but we read them to her and she nodded and smiled, clearly pleased with her present.

As I hung it on the wall later in the afternoon, I was reminded of the day three and a half years before when I went for my interview with her and saw this identical verse hanging in her room in Haarlem. I had often recalled it through the years, and here it was again, much later, in a different country, a different bedroom, and in very different circumstances. The words were a silent commentary on every day.

During the coming months, Tante Corrie slowly gained strength. Her ability to walk was not returning but there was a little movement in her right arm and leg. Her throat muscles became stronger and she was able to eat more solid food. We transferred her daily from her bed to her wheelchair, except when she was too ill for such activity.

In all the weakness, illness, and confusion, Tante Corrie retained her essential inner peace and never did those of us around her detect rebellion against God. It was not that we never saw her weep. We did. We also saw moments of frustration and an emotional debility so common in stroke patients.

For example, sometimes, for no apparent reason, Tante Corrie began to cry. At first I found this upsetting until I realized that it was part of the illness and had to be dealt with as such.

"Tante Corrie, what is the matter?"

A shaking of her head and a trembling of her thin shoulders.

"Are you in pain?"

"No."

"Are you weeping because everything is so difficult?"

"Ja!"

"Let's go to the Lord with it, Tante Corrie."

"Ja." She closed her eyes.

"Father, You know how Tante Corrie is feeling and how difficult this situation is for her. Will You send the Holy Spirit, the Comforter, now at this minute to bring help to her and to restore her joy? If there is anything we need to know in order to help her, will You show us? Thank You, Lord, in Jesus' name, Amen."

We opened our eyes. She had stopped weeping and held out her hand for a tissue. Blowing her nose firmly as if to say, "It is over," she was quiet and at peace again. She was not immune to the emotional instability that all stroke patients have to bear, but in her times of distress her relationship with the Lord Jesus was very real, and He sustained her.

In what way is she fulfilling God's will now? I asked myself, but even as I asked the question I could see part of the answer.

There had been a tremendous change in her way of life, one that could crush the spirit—but that had not happened. She was living for God. I could see no difference in the attitude of this weak and silent Tante Corrie to that of the strong speaker whom I had joined nearly three years earlier. She served Him then; she was serving Him now. Her attitude said to me, "Since this suffering has come my way I will go through it with the Lord with the same resolution I needed when I was well."

She had served Him in her youth; now she was serving Him in her old age. She had served Him in strength, now she was serving Him in weakness. She had served Him in health; she was serving Him in illness. She had served Him in her life; she was serving Him in her death. We saw how God built her up in her spirit daily, did not forsake her, provided for her, and sustained her. A new awe and respect for the preciousness of human life came into our thinking. God had made mankind in His own image. He had made Corrie ten Boom in His own image. Whether young, old, strong, weak, well, ill, she was equally precious in His sight. His view of her had not changed although in the eyes of an achievement-oriented society she may have lost her usefulness.

In the autumn, we decided to try to make her bedroom look less like a hospital room. There was nothing we could do to disguise the large iron bed, but we used colorful sheets and a blanket in soft beige that matched the walls. Medicines were kept out of sight, and we brought roses from the garden whenever—and it happened seldom—there were no bouquets sent by friends. We brought in the little brown clock with the Roman numerals and put it on top of the bookcase. She consulted it daily. Her interest in timepieces never ceased and she had not lost her ability to tell the time.

One day we discovered that the little brown clock had stopped in the night. Tante Corrie was lying on her back as I took it from the top of the bookcase and said, "I wonder what is wrong with this, Tante Corrie?"

Lotte and I both looked at it, made sure it was wound up and tried to get the pendulum started. Nothing happened.

Tante Corrie motioned with her left hand and I took the clock to her. While I supported the clock and her right hand lay useless by her side, Tante Corrie opened the back of it with her left hand, and with her long fingers made some adjustment that Lotte and I did not see. There was a confidence in the way she used her hand that made me think of her work at the watchmaker's bench at the Beje. The result of that adjustment was that the clock resumed its friendly *tick* and maintained it.

One thing that helped the room was that the red bougainvillaea outside her window was now established and bloomed prolifically casting a pink glow onto the inside walls. It had established itself firmly around the iron railings making them far less visible. Above the bougainvillaeas she could see the sky and loved to lie watching it. We brought one of the birdfeeders from the back of the house and kept it filled, and purchased another hummingbird feeder so that she could watch her favorite birds.

The days went slowly by. We heard the familiar whirring of the electric bed as we lowered it to change her position, the metallic clicking of the rails as we raised and lowered them to turn our patient, the ticking of the brown clock. Nine months passed. It was not easy for her or for us. It was very hard sometimes. There were days when the routine seemed endless and the hours seemed to last for days.

Our patient was never alone at night and had the help of two nurses, Ruth Jean who worked on weeknights and Bernice Meyer who took the weekend night duty shift.

Tante Corrie had frequent small strokes. They would be preceded by certain signs. For instance, we may have noticed a restlessness, such as an inability to get to sleep at night, downheartedness or anxiety, when frown lines would appear on her forehead, discouragement shown by a deep sigh. We learned to recognize the signs, but could never prevent the strokes.

It was not an easy commission. Lotte and I were often very tired and tense and as in any household there were disagreements. One day after we had dealt with a restless Tante Corrie, several matters of business, the telephone and visitors, the straw that broke the camel's back in the early afternoon was whether or not to give Tante Corrie a mild sedative prescribed by the doctor for days when it was very hard for her to relax. I thought very definitely that she was not so restless that she needed the medication, and Lotte thought equally definitely that she should have it. Finally we decided to give it to Tante Corrie, and it was obviously the right thing to do because she was much better and slept for a couple of hours.

Lotte and I spent the rest of the day with little conversation between the two of us. We had just finished turning Tante Corrie in the late afternoon when she looked from one to the other of us with eyes that told us that she discerned that something was wrong. I asked Elizabeth to sit with Tante Corrie for a while, and Lotte and I went to the sitting room to talk the matter through. There we asked forgiveness of each other. It was not our only disagreement, but we had a very good teacher and she taught us not to let the sun go down on our anger.

Because she had always loved to plan, and to give her the opportunity to look forward to certain events, we put as much order into the day as possible. After Bible reading, prayer, and being made ready for the day, Tante Corrie had physical therapy exercises, then a rest and a cup of coffee. She liked to hold the cup by herself with her left hand and accepted help only when she was too weak to lift it. Usually at this point she wanted to be taken in the wheelchair to the garden and enjoyed the sun and fresh air for as long as she could sit comfortably. It was an exhausting exercise, and after she had been put back to bed she rested for a while.

After this Lotte often read to her. We saw her blue eyes light up as she relived her family history from *In My Father's House, Father ten Boom—God's Man,* and her own life history in *Tramp for the Lord.* We avoided reading *The Hiding Place* and her book *A Prisoner and Yet . . .* because of the detailed reminders of concentration camp. She had told me when she was well that since she stopped traveling she thought more about her prison days. We did not want to put her in the position of reliving scenes from her past and not be able to talk about them.

Tante Corrie liked us to sit next to her and talk to her as much as possible and she still looked forward to the daily arrival of the mail, which we read to her whenever she was well enough. There were daily reports of the ways God was using her books and films in people's lives throughout the world and often news came in about how the Gospel was reaching others through the missionaries whom she support- ed financially. She followed all this with interest.

Each day when she was well enough, she received visitors. Many of them remarked to us about the peaceful atmosphere of Shalom House, and referred to Tante Corrie's undiminished spiritual gift of discernment: "Those eyes of hers . . . they looked right inside me."

Her friends were very kind to her and to us. They brought gifts of flowers and food and offered help and we took them up on their offers frequently. Lotte had many practical ideas and one was to use small, flat, soft cushions to place between Tante Corrie's ankles, under her paralyzed right arm and under her head pillow to bolster it when needed. Jane Klassen sewed several of these, about eighteen inches square, an inch thick, soft and pliable. We used up to half-a- dozen of them in her bed and in the wheelchair.

Grady and Maurine Parrott, our neighbor prayer part- ners came to the house often and visited her. The prayer meeting that had begun at their home two years earlier continued to meet every week. At the beginning the intention had been to pray specifically for prisoners. While we continued to do this we also added to our prayers the many people who wrote to Tante Corrie asking for prayer, and we prayed for Tante Corrie herself. There were usually only five of us at that weekly meeting, but how God used it to strengthen us.

Another activity that we used to fill part of our days was the viewing of the approximately 7,000 slides that Tante Corrie had taken during her journeys around the world. We set up the projector and screen, closed the drapes and set out on journeys to Africa, Russia, Japan, Korea, Indonesia, England, Canada, Holland, New Zealand, Israel, and many other countries. There was much enjoyment in this for Tante Corrie, and a lot of communication. Sometimes a picture of a particular country would trigger my memory and I would recall our evenings in the living room during our first year at Shalom House when she told me stories from her adventures around the world.

"Look, Tante Corrie, here is a picture from Ethiopia— Haile Selassie's grandchildren. Do you remember your meeting with the emperor when you were in that country? The dress code necessitated that you wear a hat and gloves for your audience with him, but you did not have either item so you borrowed them from a missionary. The hat was too big. You had to bow three times, once after entering the room, once halfway across the room, and once when you were standing in front of the emperor. You spoke to him in English, and your conversation was translated through an interpreter, although you knew that he understood English. You talked to him about the second coming of the Lord. When it was time to go you had to leave his presence walking backward and to bow three times again, once in front of him, once halfway to the door, and for a third time, again, at the door. You were afraid that the hat would fall off every time you bowed, and you used the opportunity of the second bow to locate the position of the door behind you."

Tante Corrie laughed at the memory, but she also prayed with great concern for the people of Ethiopia.

The little brown clock ticked away the hours. A year passed since the second debilitating stroke. Frequently my mind would compare her activity of previous years with her inactivity of the present. Her lips could no longer say, "Jesus is Victor," but her life could, and it did. I remembered the dream she had had several times during our first year together, when we were traveling:

"I have had that dream again."

"What dream is that, Tante Corrie?"

"In my dream I am inside a room from which I cannot escape. I am permanently there, and it is rather like a prison. While I am there, my message is still going out to the people through films and books and television."

This was literally happening now. Along with the circulation of the films and books produced at Shalom House, *The Hiding Place* movie, adapted for television, had reached a huge audience. But most amazing to me was that her message was also still being brought by her personally. She still had a great love for people, and God enabled her to communicate that love without words.

One day for example, a policeman came to Shalom House to help us with an inquiry about a disturbance in the neighborhood. He was tough, and judging by the look on his face, his was a thankless task in the main. He was interested, though, when he heard whose house he was in, told us that he had seen *The Hiding Place* movie and asked if he could visit Tante Corrie. She was not at all well that day, but knowing that she would be an encouragement to him, we asked her if she would receive him. She nodded enthusiastically, and we turned her to her left side so that she would be facing the door when he came through it. The expression on her face as he entered told him, "This is the very person I have been waiting to see." He took her thin hand between his two strong ones, got down on his knees and kissed her hand. On her behalf we started a conversation:

"How good it is to meet you."

"I have seen your movie."

"Did you understand the message of the movie that there is no pit so deep that the love of God is not deeper still?"

"Well, I saw the movie twice, so I understood something of it."

A short "conversation" followed and the policeman left, after Tante Corrie had prayed with him and had indicated that she wanted us to give him one of her books as a gift. He offered to provide any help he could should we ever need it and said he would keep in touch. We believed that the Lord used those moments in his life and that He used the countless other times when people visited her bedside.

Then, there was the teenager, Bob, who made this statement: "When I met her, such a love came from her that I immediately stopped the wrong things I was getting into under the influence of my brother."

There was Karen, the girl in her twenties, who arrived at the house late one evening after everyone had retired for the night. I recognized her as a former flower shop employee who had delivered a bouquet to Tante Corrie more than a year earlier. She wanted to talk. She had seen such life and love in Tante Corrie's eyes when she brought her the flowers that she said she would never forget it.

One and a half years passed by, the physical weakness continued, but Tante Corrie had not become too ill or too old to give or receive love.

11.

A Prisoner and Yet ...

In the autumn of 1980, a year and a half after the previous one, came a third severe stroke. The October morning progressed as usual, except that Tante Corrie did not want to get up for her session in the wheelchair. In fact, she never got up again.

Elizabeth prepared lunch at the regular time, and just as Lotte brought the lunchtray containing our three meals to her bedroom, Tante Corrie suddenly collapsed and fell to the right.

I ran to the telephone and called her internist, who was on his rounds at the nearby hospital. He must have made straight for his car, for within a few minutes he was at her bedside. She was lying limp and exhausted. The doctor told us that he thought that another stroke was in progress but that we would have to wait until the evening to be sure.

All afternoon Lotte and I watched at Tante Corrie's bedside, unable to do anything but pray for her. Her face was gray, her eyes closed, her right side unmoving. Beads of perspiration stood out on her forehead. There was a moment when I thought I could not bear to watch her suffer any longer: "Father," I prayed, "please release Tante Corrie from this long and difficult illness. She has served You for more than eighty years. May she please go home now, Lord?"

I continued to watch and to wait that afternoon for the Lord's answer. He did not answer me with "yes" or "no" or even "wait." Again, there seemed to be no answer at all.

By the end of the day the doctor informed us that there had been another stroke. Because her general condition was so much weaker than before, we thought it very unlikely that she would pull through. She lay mainly unresponsive and in a state of sleep or semi-consciousness. But as before, whenever she roused, we placed a syringe in her mouth and tried to get her to swallow a small amount of liquid.

One day, two weeks later, her skin felt dry and hot and she had begun to cough. After he had checked her that day the doctor walked with me to the sitting room while Lotte stayed with Tante Corrie. *What is he going to suggest?* I wondered. *How long can a person remain this ill?*

Out of the corner of my eye, through the sliding glass doors I could see her beloved garden. It seemed such a long time since we had last pushed Tante Corrie outside.

"I think Corrie has pneumonia," the doctor began.

"That is very serious, isn't it?" I asked.

"Yes, it can be. The time has come to make a decision. If we admit her to the hospital now, she will have to undergo the standard treatment of antibiotics, respirator, and so forth. I think she would much rather be at home in her own room, receiving care from those she knows well."

"Will the pneumonia take her life?" I asked.

"It may. If it does not, I would rather see her come out of it on her own than with the application of the measures she would need to undergo in the hospital."

The doctor left and as soon as possible Lotte and I talked the matter through. We both agreed with him that it was right to keep her home.

How often we have prayed that we will do the right thing, I thought as we turned Tante Corrie before putting out her light for the night, *and now that the time has come to make an important decision like this, the Lord has given us peace about keeping her home.*

I decided to make some detailed notes in my diary. Perhaps the day would come when I would be able to help other people in similar experiences. Everybody has to face issues of the life and death of loved ones at some time or other, and it is important to have thought these issues through in general as far as possible. Then, when a particular issue arises, as it had arisen with us, the Holy Spirit is able to give particular guidance in individual cases.

The following two months, more than any other time up to that point, convinced me that our times are in God's hands and are not dependent on the will or skill of men and women.

Tante Corrie did not fight to live, she did not fight to die. She lay in her large iron bed and took what came, not battling, but yielding. We knew this because of her attitude during the times when she opened her eyes and looked at us. Her eyes were peaceful, and they left us peaceful and with a strong sense that God was in control.

Amazingly, Tante Corrie stopped coughing and was no longer feverish. She had recovered from pneumonia without the use of antibiotics. It was remarked to me by several people that her pacemaker was keeping her alive but I questioned this. I could not help feeling that that was not the full story, because she had a demand pacemaker that functioned only when her heart dropped below a certain rate. I took her pulse several times a day and it often happened, then and in previous years, that her heart was beating on its own, above the rate of the pacemaker. For weeks, she hovered between life and death, very unresponsive, eating very little, but taking fluids through a syringe whenever conscious.

The little brown clock ticked the hours away. Outside, the bougainvillaea was clothed in its autumn green, but we could not see it as the drapes were half-closed. We turned Tante Corrie regularly and wondered how long this situation could last. How was it possible that she could be so ill and yet continue to live?

Sharon, our neighbor nurse, could not throw any light on the mystery. "With Corrie you just cannot tell," she said. "But I think that if she does recover, the problem of aphasia will be even more intensified. This stroke has probably inflicted more brain damage."

One thing I was sure of. She could not remain in this inert condition forever, not even Corrie ten Boom, as unusual as she was.

And then, one morning when I walked into her room, instead of the unresponsive figure on the iron bed, there was Tante Corrie looking at me out of her eyes. She was back! How it happened I cannot tell, but suddenly her responses were returning. She began to eat and drink small amounts more frequently, and her skin started to take on more tone over her brittle body.

So it happened that Tante Corrie made a reentrance onto life's stage against all expectation and prognosis. Sharon's prediction that the problem with aphasia may be intensified proved correct. It was much harder for Tante Corrie to understand us now and for us to understand her. Her capacity to comprehend varied with the blood supply to the brain at any given moment.

Not only had her body become very thin, but also very rigid. We sat her up by raising the head of the electric bed, but we had to do it slowly and in stages as the raising of her head tended to cause faintness. It had been possible to get her into her wheelchair, with much difficulty, before this stroke. Now it could not be done. This was for me one of the hardest things of all. On many a day when the sun was shining and the roses were in full bloom I wished with all my heart that we could get her outside. If only that large bed could be rolled down the corridor, but it was too wide. I had to accept the circumstances as they were. I remembered again her dream: "I am in a room from which I cannot escape. . . ." It had become literally true.

In an effort to try and understand this new turn of events, I talked to the doctor about a month after Tante Corrie's rally.

"What do you think we can expect now?" I asked him as I accompanied him to the front door.

"With Corrie that is hard to say," was his reply.

"What do you think her life expectancy could be?"

"It is not possible to know. She could die as we are standing here talking, or she could live for some time yet."

How gracious the Lord is that He does not normally reveal the future to us, but shows us the way to go one step at a time so that we learn to rely on Him from day to day. It is good that none of us knew that at eighty-eight years of age more than two years of complete physical helplessness were still ahead of Tante Corrie.

Lotte and I came to realize that Shalom House had become a professional care unit.

"Why don't you consider putting Corrie in a home?" was a question that reached us more than once. It was not a question we ever considered, but the fact was that we were now running a little nursing home of our own. We well realized that many people have no choice but to put their loved ones in a nursing home when they become too ill to be cared for at home. Tante Corrie was in a position of having a home whose layout made it possible to be looked after there, and she had staff and helpers, many on a voluntary basis, who were able to meet her needs.

The staff at Shalom House underwent some changes in the months after the third severe stroke. Housekeeper Elizabeth left to get married and Arlene Newberry came to take her place. Young and with a deceptively fragile build, like Lotte's, Arlene took over the running of the house—laundry, shopping, cooking, care of the outside and inside plants, ordering and collecting of special equipment and prescriptions, and helping with Tante Corrie's care when needed. Also in common with Lotte she had some ingenious practical ideas.

Sharon moved with her family to another part of California. We were very sorry to lose her and wondered who the Lord would send in her place. Shortly afterward, Barbara Wells came into our lives when I met her on a visit to the local hospital. She volunteered her services and told us to call her whenever we needed her. With her Irish heritage, sense of fun, and very able professional manner, she was a welcome addition to our team of six night nurses, Bernice and Ruth being the other members.

Because of her confining circumstances, it was even more important that Tante Corrie's room become as attractive as possible. Night nurse Bernice often appeared on the doorstep during the daytime, too; she was never without a vase of flowers and sometimes two or three. Under Tante Corrie's direction, Lotte placed hundreds of photographs on the bedroom walls. She indicated to Lotte the point on the wall where she wanted each photograph to be placed until the walls were covered.

The plodding routine became almost numbing. And yet, something began to take place that set this phase of Tante Corrie's illness in a very special category. For there were times when heaven seemed very near.

One evening, while I was working in the office, Lotte was sitting next to Tante Corrie's bed before the night nurse arrived. Tante Corrie liked it when Lotte held her hand. Lotte was leaning forward, her left hand in Tante Corrie's. The drapes were closed, the room was in darkness except for a low night light on a small table at the foot of the bed. We tried to keep the room as clean-smelling as possible with lots of fresh air, but, nevertheless, it still sometimes had an antiseptic smell, rather like a hospital room. As Lotte sat there in the half-dark she was suddenly, for a few seconds, enveloped by a beautiful scent that she could only describe as "something like the scent of orange blossoms."

She came to tell me, and I immediately investigated the citrus trees outside. But the only one with any flowers was much too far away for its scent to have wafted into Tante Corrie's room. Besides, I had not smelled it in the office, which was nearer the garden, and, as Lotte pointed out, it was not exactly orange blossom, but a very fine scent, orange blossom being the nearest she could come to describing it.

Tante Corrie was asleep and had not noticed it. We concluded that the Lord had given Lotte a little foretaste of heaven.

There were other times, too, when heaven was tangibly very near. It seemed that if only a curtain could be lifted we would see inside. Tante Corrie loved it when we talked about heaven with her: "Yet I am always with you; you hold me by my right hand. You guide me with your counsel, and afterward you will take me into glory."

"Now we know that if the earthly tent we live in is destroyed, we have a building from God, an eternal house in heaven, not built by human hands."

Even the music, which we had kept regularly in our schedule, seemed to take on a more important function. Each afternoon about 4:30 p.m., I took two old Dutch hymnals from the bookcase, handed one to Lotte and we started singing one of the old Dutch hymns with which Tante Corrie had grown up. Ever since the first stroke it had been possible for her to sing sometimes. When she recognized the melody and joined in, the words sometimes followed. Even now she joined in whenever she could. There was her father's favorite:

"I cannot live without Thee, Thou Jesus, my Lord, and I am Thine forever; be Thy name adored," and many others. We usually sang for about half an hour and we all enjoyed it.

Lotte sat next to Tante Corrie's bed one day while she was on her right side facing the window. They had been talking about the fact that Jesus was Victor even in these very difficult circumstances.

"I can't think of a hymn on the subject 'Jesus is Victor,'" said Lotte to Corrie. "There really should be one. Perhaps the Lord will give us one." Tante Corrie immediately closed her eyes and prayed.

A few days later, the Lord gave Lotte a hymn of several verses, in Dutch, which she translated into German and English, and which we sang to a seventeenth-century Dutch tune. Tante Corrie was so happy with it, doubtless, also, because she had been instrumental in its being written in that she had prayed for it. She liked us to sing it to her often:

> "Jesus Christ alone is Victor
>   now and in eternity!
> In His sovereignty He reigneth,
>   great in power and majesty."

To me, it was as if Tante Corrie were standing at the doorway to heaven, and our feeble human voices were only echoes of the angelic anthems.

And then there was the very unusual occurrence at Christmas, a year after the third severe stroke. Tante Corrie was feeling very unwell, and although there was much peace in Shalom House, the whole team was tired. Outside in the world around us people were busily preparing for the season. There were colored lights on many of the houses, and the atmosphere was full of activity, very different to the scene inside Tante Corrie's bedroom.

Ruth, whose evening knock was always welcome, said to me a couple of days before Christmas Eve, "You know that verse in Hebrews, 'Are not all angels ministering spirits sent to serve those who will inherit salvation?'"

"Yes," I said, wondering what was coming next.

"Well, I think that Tante Corrie has angels in her bedroom."

"What do you mean?"

It seemed that every evening recently, Ruth had witnessed a shadow cast on the bed as if somebody had passed along beside the night light at the foot of the bed. But no one else was there. And there was a strong sense of comfort and peace in the room at the same time. "I think it's an angel," she concluded.

"Really," I said. "That is very interesting," not adding what I was really thinking: Ruth was seeing things. Yet Ruth was a practical woman, having grown up on a farm, and she saw things very simply. In that way she reminded me of Tante Corrie. It was not like her to be imagining angels. *She must be very tired,* I concluded.

The next day, however, Lotte mentioned that she, too, had seen a shadow in Tante Corrie's room. There was something wrong with the bulb of the night light, I decided, and exchanged it for a new one.

"Have you seen any shadows in Tante Corrie's room?" I asked Bernice when she appeared for weekend duty a couple of nights later.

"As a matter of fact I have," she replied. "At first I thought it was headlights from cars on the street. But that can't be it, because there have always been cars outside and their lights have not caused this kind of shadow."

The next day it was again my turn at Tante Corrie's bedside. In the near dark, I wondered if I would see an angel. Surely they could not all have imagined it. For quite a while I saw nothing unusual.

But when I had stopped looking and was sitting quietly next to Tante Corrie, I saw what the others had seen. There was a shadow in the room—not a dark hovering thing, but, if it is possible, a bright shadow. And at once I was overcome by a sense of comfort and peace, like the times when you do not realize you have been tense, but, upon heaving a sigh of relaxation, realize you were.

When we talked about it later, we agreed that God was reminding us that we were not alone as we accompanied Tante Corrie—as far as we were permitted—through a very long valley of the shadow of death.

After Christmas Tante Corrie rallied a little and we pressed on with the routine. There were days when my back ached, I was tired and dispirited, and did not feel like continuing. Our team of six grew very close because deeper relationships are forged in difficult times, I was discovering, than in easier ones.

It may not always have been smooth sailing, but Arlene kept Shalom House running and there was little she could not do. Her slight figure belied a certain strength and practicality. She fixed light fuses, broken shelves, and screen doors with effortless speed.

One task that could not be accomplished very speedily, however, was the preparing of blended meals. Arlene knew exactly which consistency Tante Corrie's damaged throat could handle, but it took a great deal of time to prepare potatoes, vegetables, and meat each day and blend them all. There had to be a more practical way of having meals on hand, she thought, than her present method of daily preparation.

Then she remembered a suggestion she had read years before. She took three ice cube trays and poured into one the blended potatoes, into another blended carrots, and into the third blended chicken. When the substances had frozen she removed them from the trays, put them into containers suitable for freezing, and labeled them. Soon the freezer compartment of the refrigerator was stocked with blended foods, all clearly marked. Two cubes of frozen potatoes, one cube of vegetable, and one cube of meat when heated were all that Tante Corrie could usually manage at one time, and from then on it was easy for Lotte and me to prepare meals when Arlene was off-duty on weekends.

By no means did Lotte and I feel alone in our commission. Tante Corrie and we had some wonderful helpers. There were many good friends, neighbors, and volunteers who prayed regularly, bore the burdens with us spiritually, advised us, did odd jobs around the house, did extra typing, brought food, flowers, and gifts, ran errands, and undertook sewing assignments. This kind of cooperation was unique in my experience. I had never seen anything like it before.

Tante Corrie's night nurses, housekeeper, and visiting registered nurse had never known their patient when she was well. I was sometimes a little suspicious of the admiration in which I held Tante Corrie, because of my position as her constant companion and the fact that I had known her when she was in the full swing of work and ministry. But I began to see the same respect emerging in people who had never known her before.

One afternoon, Bernice and Barbara were relaxing at the oval table in the dining room. I went to the kitchen to fix tea and a plate of cookies, and as I did so I could hear their conversation. It went something like this:

"What is the thing you most appreciated about Tante Corrie when you first met her?" said Barbara to Bernice.

"One thing I particularly remember," Bernice replied, "is that she accepted me just as I was and let me minister to her needs with a very helpful spirit."

"I was struck by the immediacy of her prayers," said Barbara. "Whenever a request or a problem was mentioned she closed her eyes, took my hand, and began to pray. Very direct. She really cares about us all."

I joined them at the table and was glad to have this insight into how the other team members saw her. So I was not the only one who was so deeply impressed by her relationship with the Lord. How I wished there was a way for the love of God that came through Tante Corrie in such difficult circumstances to become more widely known.

But her influence did extend further than her immediate team. There was, for instance, the gardener, an Oriental gentleman to whom it was not particularly easy to talk. For one thing, it was hard to shout above the noise of the lawnmower, which started at the moment he arrived and continued relentlessly until shortly before he left. There were occasions when Arlene, Lotte, and I individually had followed him as he plunged through the garden with the lawn mower, trying to ask him to take care of a certain item. He seemed to ignore us. We didn't blame him. He knew his business, kept the lawns neat and the shrubs tidy and probably did not appreciate the landscaping suggestions of the three of us.

It had been a long time since he had seen Tante Corrie because even when she had been well enough to go to the garden in her wheelchair we had not usually taken her at a time when the gardener plus equipment was present.

One day I heard the familiar roar of the lawn mower when I took a tray to the kitchen.

"What do you think?" said Arlene. "Shall we invite the gardener to say hello to Tante Corrie?"

"Well," I said doubtfully, "we are not very successful at talking to him so I am not sure he would want to. But ask him if you like, because I think Tante Corrie is well enough to see him."

Arlene went outside and before I could unload the tray and get back to the bedroom, there was the gardener standing inside the front door, wiping his hands on his pants.

"I'm not very tidy," he apologized.

I told him it did not matter and that I would tell Tante Corrie he was coming. She looked pleased when I told her of the gardener's visit. We positioned her on her left side and covered her with a pretty blue shawl that Lotte had made. She looked very frail lying against her pillows, but her eyes were fixed on the door. Her expression was about to tell the gardener: "There is nobody in the world I would rather see than you."

From my position just inside the bedroom I saw the gardener coming down the corridor. His face was expressionless. As soon as he rounded the door of her bedroom, however, and his brown eyes met Tante Corrie's blue ones, there was an immediate dynamic contact between them. I had never seen him so animated. His face broke into the biggest smile I had ever seen him give and she returned it.

"Hi!" he said, very loudly, walking quickly to the bed and taking her hand.

Lotte and I helped them to communicate for a few minutes and then I accompanied him to the front door.

"I could hear his greeting all the way back here in the kitchen," said Arlene, "the man has got a heart after all."

Even when she cannot speak, she can reach people that we cannot reach, I thought. From that time on the gardener paid extra special attention to the part of the garden that lay in her field of vision, trimming the bougainvillaea regularly.

On as many days as her strength would allow, Tante Corrie continued to receive visitors and somehow often picked up needs not expressed by them. One afternoon, Vuryl, Tante Corrie's handyman professor, and Jane, his wife, came to the door with Kelly and her two younger brothers. I remembered their first visit when we had just come to Shalom House five years before.

The youngest boy had been a toddler then; now he was a

little man, very serious and holding a kitten. So were his
brother and sister. They went carefully and quietly to Tante
Corrie's bedside. She lay facing the window and was
delighted with the children and the kittens. She had always
liked cats. I wondered if these kittens reminded her of her cat
at the Beje who had been given the lengthy and probably
well-deserved name of Maher-Shalal-Hash-Baz ("Quick to
the plunder, swift to the spoil," from Isaiah 8:1). Tante
Corrie gave the children and their kittens her full attention.
Yet for some reason, she particularly focused on the kitten in
the hands of the youngest child. We found out later that the
little boy had been especially thrilled by this, because he had
really wanted to hold one of the other kittens. His older
brother and sister had taken precedence over him and he had
shed a few tears about it. It seemed as if Tante Corrie knew
that his kitten should have an extra stroke or two. She had
sensed the child's need.

The days passed on. They held many personal encour-
agements from the Lord, such as the morning when I was
washing Tante Corrie's feet and experienced the greatest
sense of fulfillment that I had never known. It caused me to
thank God. He had taken an impractical person and given
her a very practical ministry. That day I remembered how,
early in the morning of the day of Tante Corrie's first stroke, I
had read John 13:14:

"Now that I, your Lord and Teacher, have washed your
feet, you also should wash one another's feet." He had
allowed that latter part to become literally true in my life and
as I realized this, at the same moment I became aware that
servanthood is the very highest calling. And even as I thought
it I knew it was true that I had a very long way to go in
learning to be a true servant of the Lord.

And another insight occurred to me. Tante Corrie had
identified herself with so many of those whom she had helped.

She had been in prison and could therefore speak with authority to prisoners. But now it was working as it were the other way around. When she was young she had clubs for mentally retarded people not knowing what it felt like to have brain damage. Now she herself was brain-damaged, and was identifying with the mentally retarded in a new way.

But the real identification was with the Lord Jesus. How I wished I knew what He was saying to her. Sometimes there was a look of longing and peace on Tante Corrie's face and her expression was rather introspective and reflective. Was she thinking about her previous imprisonment? Was there any comparison between that and this present suffering?

One day as Lotte sat beside her bed, Tante Corrie pointed toward the wall.

"Do you want to put up some more photographs, Corrie?"

"No."

"Do you mean something is wrong with the wall?"

"No."

Tante Corrie closed her eyes, prayed in her own manner of using any sounds that came, said "Amen" clearly and looked up at Lotte.

"Are you telling us something about the Lord, Corrie?"

"Ja!"

"What is it, has He been speaking to you?"

"Ja!"

"Has He encouraged you? Has He shown you something of His glory?"

"Ja, ja!"

We longed to know more, but what Tante Corrie had seen or heard remained a secret between her and the Lord.

In the two years following the second stroke, it seemed that Tante Corrie was being withdrawn from us more and more into the presence of the Lord. It became harder to reach her. Sometimes when she was resting with her eyes closed, or asleep, while I sat next to her, her hand in mine, I began to pray for her silently under my breath. It happened repeatedly that as I prayed for her, Tante Corrie opened her eyes and looked directly at me. I wondered how the Lord was answering my prayers for her. She could not have heard them, but a result was that the Lord gave communication between her and me.

We still have you, Tante Corrie, I thought, *and yet we do not have you. It is almost as if you are living in the foyer of heaven.*

In the summer of 1982, nearly two years after the last stroke, a telephone call was received from Loren Cunningham, friend of Tante Corrie's and leader of Youth with a Mission, asking if he could visit her. He was in our area in connection with the launching of a mission ship. I knew it was a very busy time for him and that there must be a special reason for his wanting to come. We agreed on a day and time.

A few days later, Loren and his wife Darlene arrived at Shalom House and I led them into the sitting room. It was a beautiful sunny day and I could feel the warm breeze through the open sliding doors. The roses were in full bloom, the sparrows were chattering around the birdfeeder. Lotte was with Tante Corrie, Arlene was busy in the kitchen.

Loren, Darlene, and I took our seats under the portrait of Father ten Boom, and I told them about Tante Corrie's general condition. It was good to talk to them. I knew that Loren was a spiritually sensitive man.

"I wanted to talk to you," said Loren, "about a commission which I believe the Lord has given me." He leaned forward. *What a kind face he has,* I thought. His photograph had decorated Tante Corrie's walls on many occasions throughout the last years. "But first of all, I need to fill you in with a bit of the background. Did Tante Corrie ever tell you that ten years ago she asked me to pray for her on her birthday that God would give new direction in her ministry?"

"Yes." I replied, "I remember her telling me that."

"I prayed as she had asked," continued Loren, "but I also felt led to pray for something else—that God would add ten years to her life. Those ten years have now passed with her last birthday, and I believe God is asking me to pray on behalf of the church for her full healing in glory."

"How do you know that, Loren?"

He replied with another question: "Have you ever asked the Lord to take Tante Corrie to heaven?"

"Yes," I replied, remembering my urgent prayer at the beginning of the last stroke. "He did not do it, nor did He seem to answer me."

"You know," said Loren, "it is very hard to pray for the homegoing of somebody you love, and the people who are closest to those suffering may rarely be asked to do it. It is harder for them to be able to know the right time to pray. It is easier for somebody much further removed. I believe that the right time has come now to pray for her homegoing." He said it very gently.

It was quiet for a moment in the sitting room. I could tell that Darlene was praying hard.

"Shall we ask Tante Corrie first if you may pray like that?" I asked.

I left the sitting room and walked up the corridor to Tante Corrie's bedroom. Slowly I explained to her that Loren was coming to see her and that he wanted to pray for her homegoing on behalf of the church. She nodded. Lotte and I believed she understood.

Lying facing the window, Tante Corrie received her visitor. She smiled and held out her hand to Loren as he entered the room. He greeted her and held her thin hand between his two large ones for a moment, then took his Bible and read to her a short portion from Luke 13 about the crippled woman who was healed on the Sabbath day:

"When Jesus saw her, he called her forward and said to her, 'Woman, you are set free from your infirmity.' Then he put his hands on her, and immediately she straightened up and praised God."

Then Loren prayed a short and simple prayer, on behalf of all the church, asking God to set Tante Corrie free from her infirmity and to release her to complete healing in glory. Tante Corrie smiled and nodded in agreement and Loren took leave of her.

I walked behind him down the corridor. There had been a relaxed authority in his short prayer. I thought about Loren's comments on my closeness to the situation. Was that why it seemed the Lord had not heard my own prayer for her release? Had it not been the right time then? Was it the right time now?

I accompanied Loren and Darlene to the front door. Before we said goodbye to each other Loren said: "I do not know when the Lord will take her, but I believe it will be this year."

Lotte and I, as we thought and prayed about it that evening, believed that if God were speaking specifically through Loren, He would take Tante Corrie to Himself on or before her next birthday.

Was the long wait about to come to a close? There was only one thing I knew for sure. Tante Corrie had been waiting for a very long time and had spent that time in the most creative way I could imagine.

12.

A Time to Die

During the coming months and especially in the new year of 1983, Tante Corrie became ever weaker. It had now been six years since her move to her own home and two and a half years since her last stroke.

One morning while Lotte was making breakfast in the kitchen, I sat next to Tante Corrie's bed. She was lying on her right side, dressed in her blue nightgown with the white lace edging. She was very thin—literally skin and bone. There was nothing she could do without assistance. I held her hand, and together we looked at the birds for a few moments as they vied for a place on the perch of the feeder. I turned back toward Tante Corrie and saw that she was looking not at the birds, but at me. The only words I can use to describe the look on her face is that her eyes were full of love. As I received that look, I too became full of love. And I marveled again at the communication that is possible in silence.

Suddenly she surprised me by saying a word in Dutch: "*Blij*" ("Happy," more literally, "joyful").

"Are you happy, Tante Corrie?"

"Ja."

She made a certain movement with her mouth, which I had come to recognize as a desire to sing. I began to sing one of her favorite Dutch hymns and she joined in very slowly, but as quickly as her old heart would allow:

"*Prijst de Heer met blijde galmen.*"
"Praise God with waves of joy.

183

You, my soul, have such cause to be thankful.
For as long as I live I will dedicate my psalms to His
     praise,
As long as I see light I will extol God in my song."

Tante Corrie's condition deteriorated markedly. Slowly, like a candle going out, she was slipping away from us. Light hurt her eyes. Her appetite was practically gone. Lotte continued to read the Bible even though Tante Corrie often appeared not to hear. The members of the staff of Shalom House intensified their efforts to keep our patient comfortable. Night nurses worked many extra hours. Barbara came daily after her work at the hospital.

April 15 arrived but Tante Corrie was not aware that it was her ninety-first birthday. She was in a semicomatose state all day. Lots of beautiful flowers were delivered, and there were written and telephoned messages. At about 2:30 p.m. I answered a knock at the door and discovered Grady and Maurine with a bunch of yellow rosebuds.

"We know that Tante Corrie has lots of flowers," Grady said, "but we could not come empty-handed on her birthday."

Quietly they entered her room and we told our unconscious patient about the presence of her visitors and their gift. We wondered if she understood. An hour later we sang to her a little of two Dutch hymns, one about the lovely name of Jesus, and the other, "Praise God with waves of joy." We told her that we loved her, but what was much more important, that nothing could separate her from the love of God in Jesus Christ. She opened her eyes and we knew that she had understood.

Early evening arrived, bringing Bernice for the night-nurse shift. Throughout the evening Tante Corrie's condition worsened. She was now completely unconscious and her limbs were very cold. Whatever we did we could not succeed in warming her hands and feet.

Bernice was standing by Tante Corrie's bed as Lotte and I left the room late in the evening. The lamp in the corner of the room was burning, Tante Corrie was lying on her back. I closed the door.

Lotte went to her bedroom and I went to mine, leaving the door ajar. Knowing how very serious her condition was, I listened for any unusual sound.

It was 10:30 p.m., and I decided to read Isaiah 53 before going to sleep. Climbing into bed, I piled several pillows under my shoulders and took out my King James Bible. As I read, propped up on my pillows, I saw that there were many ways during these past years in which Tante Corrie had identified with the sufferings of the Lord Jesus.

. . . *There is no beauty that we should desire him.* The same was true of her. Physically she was reduced to practically nothing.

. . . *As a sheep before her shearers is dumb, so he openeth not his mouth.* He had been silent for her sake and mine. And she had been silent, too. Silent because she had to be, but silent also in the attitude of her will. She had not protested.

As I meditated on these things I heard a sound from Tante Corrie's bedroom. Bernice had opened the door.

Grabbing my robe I jumped out of bed, opened my bedroom door wide, and ran up the corridor into Tante Corrie's room. The lamp was still burning in the corner, throwing light on Bernice and on the fragile little soldier on her iron chariot. Running to her side I saw that Tante Corrie's breathing pattern had changed. Quickly I ran to the wall separating Tante Corrie's room from Lotte's, knocked on it, and returned to the bed. Lotte joined us a few seconds later.

The three of us stood next to Tante Corrie as she

breathed for the last time and very peacefully went to the Lord Jesus.

There were no heavenly revelations. The room was quiet and peaceful just before she left us. It was quiet and peaceful after she left us.

I turned and looked at the little brown clock. It was three minutes to eleven in the evening of her birthday, April 15, 1983, ninety-one years to the day of her birth and exactly on time.

Epilogue

Two years after Tante Corrie's homegoing, about the time of her birthday, I visited her grave. It took me a few minutes to locate it, there being nothing to distinguish it, at a distance, from so many others. When I had last seen it, the patch of turf was obviously fresh, different in color from the rest of the grass. Now the grave was no longer new; it blended with the grass all around it. Only the inscription spoke of the life and joy that had been Tante Corrie:

Corrie ten Boom
1892-1983
Jesus Is Victor

The memorial park was still and peaceful. A slight breeze stirred the trees. I thought about Tante Corrie as she now really was—happier and more alive than she had ever been, in the presence of the Lord. Only He knew how many lives she had influenced for His sake, not least mine.

I journeyed in my mind back to the time two years before when, after helping to close Shalom House, I set out for my homeland. Although some of my relatives had been to visit me in the States, it had been nearly six years since I had had the opportunity to be in England. Now I hoped for a few months' vacation before embarking on whatever work I would be led to next.

As the plane circled lower and lower over England's

green countryside, I had grown more eager to see my family again. My parents had always encouraged me in my work and had met my plane at London airport on countless occasions. With a profound sense of relief that a difficult commission was over, I passed through customs, collected my suitcases and made for the exit, where I knew my family would be waiting.

They were indeed waiting, but I could see at once that something was very wrong, for my mother was seated in a wheelchair. I had known that she had been having difficulty walking and that a specialist had diagnosed a bone disease, but it was a shock to find her so immobile. She had always been a much-loved and extremely active member of the nursing staff of our local hospital in Hastings, East Sussex, from which she had recently retired.

A few days after my arrival, Mother had to take to her bed. I found myself applying to her care many of the things I had learned while looking after Tante Corrie. As the weeks passed and her condition worsened, we found that her illness was, in fact, terminal cancer. I was amazed at, and so very thankful for, the timing involved. For six years I had been unable to go to England. Now I was there at the very time Mother needed me most.

Again and again as I went through those strange and difficult months, I remembered the lovely Delft blue plate in Shalom House with its words, *My times are in your hands*. They truly were. Here was another indelible proof: God was sovereign and He was in control.

I remembered this as day after day I applied to my mother's nursing care what I had learned at Tante Corrie's side both spiritually and physically. Mother was so happy to have me with her, and it brought me much joy to see her surprise at watching her impractical daughter involved in nursing care. More than that, she could see that my attitude had changed. She had loved Tante Corrie very much and we talked about her often. Mother saw clearly that she had a different daughter from the one who had gone to join Corrie ten Boom seven-and-a-half years previously.

"Tante Corrie set out to change you," she said one day, with evident pride. "And she did."

Eight months after Tante Corrie's homegoing, my mother died. It was the darkest moment of my life. Again the Lord brought to mind Isaiah 53, as He had at the time of Tante Corrie's homegoing—"Surely he has borne our griefs and carried our sorrows." Deep sorrow was well-known to the Lord Jesus Christ. He had borne this for me and He was sharing it with me. I entered into a new and deeper fellowship with Him. He had been here before. He had died for this grief. It would not crush me.

And it did not. My mind returned to the present in the peaceful memorial park. I felt very rich. The Lord Jesus had proved Himself mighty in very difficult circumstances of my life.

"It is not so much what happens, but how we take it, that is important," Tante Corrie had often told me. Through the hard circumstances of the last years of her life, the Lord had shown me a paradox: The deepest fellowship with Him lies in not resisting when suffering comes our way, but in going through it resolutely with Him.